ISLAMIC FINANCE

Tom Spoors

ISBN 978-1-234-56789-1

CONTENTS

Foreword

In April 2013, I handed a short report on Islamic Finance to my former employer; he read it, praised its style and asked me to turn it into a short book. I did and he, for whatever reasons employers do, did nothing with it. That happens at work! So I put the book to one side in September of the same year, waiting for the courage to publish it later. That time arrived when my employment status changed just after New Year 2014.

My employer's company is now bankrupt and it would be very satisfying if the book could make any sales let alone a profit. Repaying honest, hard work is what a finance system of any sort should facilitate. Our current system appears to be flawed.

I did not have in mind to write and publish a book. Throughout my career almost all of my written work has been for internal company consumption or it has been training and educational material generated for specific customers in the different domains in which I have worked.

At the start, my knowledge of Islamic Finance matched what we often call that of the so-called intelligent layperson. In this case a non-Muslim intelligent layperson. For most of us this may be nothing more than an awareness of the prohibition on Riba - interest as we know it. Perhaps even less. As you'll become aware if you read on, a believing Muslim is forbidden from gaining an excess on the original amount of any loan (monetary or otherwise) based solely on the passage of time.

It is not, however, necessary to be an expert in a subject before writing an interesting and relevant book about it. Indeed, Benjamin Disraeli is quoted as saying:

> **The best way to become acquainted with a subject is to write a book about it.**[1]

An outsider can bring a fresh perspective to a subject, approaching it differently when compared to other authors who have an in-depth understanding of particular aspects of the subject. It is also true that the best way to learn a subject is to read and reflect. This is after all how we recognise expertise is many areas.

My background is in science and technical communication and this book is written from a humanist perspective. I use humanist in the British sense of a philosophy that does not require the presence of a supernatural deity in order to find and do good in the world. Good ideas, and there are many in the field of Islamic Finance, are everywhere.

You would, however, have to be somewhat disconnected from the real world not to have noticed that much of the debate around religion and society has become polarised over recent years. There are, no doubt, good sociological reasons why that may be true and it's not my intention to address any of those issues in this book. One effect of this has been that good ideas from

---

[1] http://www.quotationspage.com/quote/23684.html accessed 14 August 2013

whatever place they derive are often ignored, ridiculed or result in outpourings of anger and even violence commensurate only with what people believe about the source of the ideas themselves and not what the ideas are proposing. This is a form of argument called *ad mentem* as opposed to *ad hominem*. How we, as a global community, develop from this situation is anyone's guess but the spread of ideas that we can all begin to accept, however they are disseminated in this world of instant communication continues, from my perspective, to be the best way forward. I'm sure many will disagree.

On a personal level I am not a Muslim (and I do not confess to any creed based on a supernatural deity), nor am I a professionally-qualified finance expert. In preparing to write this book over the last year, I have read a lot and had interesting conversations with knowledgeable people in the domains of finance, history, religion and Islam in particular. The resulting book is a mixture of ideas that develop from these perspectives alongside my background in physical and biological sciences. It is not an analysis of how Islamic banks work and I have argued against some of the claims made by some of the authors where I felt that was necessary. The style in which I have constructed my arguments and described the major ideas behind money, finance and Islam is my personal view and I hope it is a useful contribution to the debate even if it cannot replace a solid education and appropriate training in the subject.

Introduction

The aim of this short book is to answer some questions on Islamic Finance. These questions are listed at the end of this introduction. To help answer those questions I will try to describe as simply as possible the philosophy, ideas and the practical implementation of Islamic Finance.

Islamic Finance (IF) is Shari'ah-based, that is, it is a system that is based on Islamic law. By the efforts of Islamic scholars and especially the jurists over centuries, but more especially over the last 50 years, it has become a religiously, legally and financially coherent system whose aim is to provide an alternative to the conventional western system of finance for those who would want to use it. It has at its base, the words of the Islamic Holy Book, the Quran, the various hadith (commentaries on the words of the Islamic prophet, Mohammed), Sunnah and Fiqh (the art of Islamic jurisprudence).

The present IF movement grew from a desire to improve social justice from the grass roots upwards in Egypt. As the price of oil has increased, various nascent IF institutions have been able to use as seed money the petrodollars entering Middle-Eastern Islamic economies as a result of the industrialised West's thirst for oil. The professed long-term aim is to allow the billions of believing Muslims to use a system of financing that complies with the teachings of the Holy Quran. Those pushing to develop the system believe there is a genuine desire among Muslims to have Shari'ah-compliant financing available for all aspects of their economic lives. That means a system for over two billion people.

In writing this book, I have relied on four main written sources and I will introduce each one as I refer to it for the first time. The first book is university-level text written by Dr Muhammed Ayub called Introduction to Islamic Finance.[2] In the introduction to his book, Ayub expresses some surprise at the slow pace of some of the developments in implementing Islamic Finance and he tries throughout to make it clear why all Muslims should seek to adopt IF in their lives. He hopes that it is just a matter of better explanation and awareness.

The best known aspect of Islamic Finance (the interdiction on the charging of excess over principal (Riba)) allows Ayub to make the following telling quote[3]:

> *Almost all Muslims believe that any involvement in Riba –*
> *taking, giving, witnessing and even documenting Riba-based*
> *transactions – is a great sin that is tantamount to waging war*
> *with Allah (SWT[4]) and his Prophet (pbuh)[5]*

---

[2] Dr Muhammad Ayub was, at the time of writing his book, the Director of Training, Development and Shari'ah Aspects at the Institute of Islamic Banking and Insurance (IIBI) London. His book is written mainly from a Pakistani perspective

[3] Ayub, Muhammed (2007) John Wiley London p433

[4] Subhanahu Wa Ta'ala," or "Glory to Him, the Exalted."

[5] pbuh = "peace be unto him"

Whether that belief of Ayub's is true or not, Ayub's frustration at the slow development of Islamic Finance in the world is evident (he is writing in 2007)[6]:

> ... why, despite the lapse of over three decades since the start of the Islamic finance movement in the modern age, is the share of Islamic banking in the financial system 1.5% in Indonesia, 2.2% in Pakistan, 12% in Malaysia and 24% in Bahrain? Bahrain is the hub of Islamic banking, where a lot of work has been done in finalizing the Shari'ah standards for Islamic modes, innovation in Shari'ah-compliant products, providing a suitable regulatory framework for Islamic banks and the establishment of an Islamic capital market. If so much preparatory work has been accomplished, why has the whole system not been transformed on a Shari'ah-compliant basis and why is a vast majority of the Muslim population still involved in waging war with Allah and His holy Prophet?

Most of the non-Muslim people that I have spoken to while researching for this book and who claim to know anything at all about Islamic Finance 'know' about this aspect of not charging 'interest'. Unfortunately, many, if not most, of them then go on to dismiss it with claims about how Islamic banks just find different ways to charge customers without **calling** it interest. I hope that at the end of this book any reasonable reader will clearly understand and accept the distinction between profit (cost-plus) generated by taking any kind of genuine business risk and interest generated merely because one has money and the Earth turns on its axis. Under Shari'ah there is a genuine desire to avoid any possible charges of Riba. However, whenever human beings and their creation money come together, best intentions are often not enough. Whether this system is any more ethical or more likely to generate happier people or allow genuine improvements in the socio-economic well-being of billions of human beings is an open question.

Like any finance system, there are a lot of details to understand. These issues, being related to money and its creation, use and distribution are necessarily complex although the basic ideas are straightforward. Money and its use has legal, ethical, technical, practical and emotional implications and intellectual efforts have to be constantly made to arrive at a useful, equitable, just, comprehensible and honest solution that will serve the global population into the future.

Western Finance appears to have no Socio-Economic Aim

Unfortunately, the created world of "high finance" is complex, fast-moving and for the vast majority of people the financial system is nothing more than a casino where the rich play with people's money and when they lose they persuade politicians that it is the poor who have to pay for their game.

---

[6] op cit

Certainly, to most people the rules of the game don't seem to have changed since the current crisis was triggered in 2007 and, it appears, no one has or will be held accountable either.

Nothing it seems changes and who would have believed, "that the lives of billions were of less consequence than a decimal point on the stock exchanges of the world"[7]. The modern western system is not a place for the faint-hearted or the ignorant but if it has a socio-economic aim beyond keeping the poorer countries poor then it is not obvious to a large number of knowledgeable commentators let alone members of the increasingly aware publics of many countries. No doubt there are those working hard to change things and the lives of many have been improved considerably, there is still much work to be done.

Islamic Finance has a religious underpinning with social justice and equity as the declared core of the system. It is an area of active research and development by Islamic scholars and jurists alongside expert economists and financiers who are themselves Muslims. They are all trying to create a system that can deliver the results of the conventional financial system without using any of the prohibited (under Shari'ah) elements of that system. Despite, the religious restrictions it remains a game played by human beings, with all the difficulties that that entails.

This book is broken down into four parts and fourteen chapters. The first four chapters discuss the main ideas behind the world of finance. The ideas of money and trade and how to ensure that any exchange is useful to both sides extends back into human history. The first chapter traces a plausible story of how we developed from hunter-gatherers bartering spare items through to shell traders and on to city-based civilizations. These civilizations relied heavily on the slave labour of conquered enemies and it was the religious temple banks that controlled enormous resources in the form of food and its source of production, land. They developed financial systems based on lending money out at interest and used financial 'products' that would not be out of place in the modern Western system.

The story continues with the religions of the 'Book' and how usury (the charging of any amount of interest) was viewed in the Talmud, the Old Testament, the Gospels and the Quran. The struggle against usurers continued throughout the development of Christian thought in the Middle and late Middle Ages and includes various Papal encyclicals, bulls and the philosophical notions of the Scholastics. During the same epoch, from the 7th century on, the spread and growth of Islam across the Arabian Peninsula resulted in a mercantile empire where the charging of interest was forbidden and where trading for profit was a God-given duty as long as it served social justice.

The story then transfers to the beginning of the modern financial system and traces the problems of that system to the point where the World's reserve

---

[7] 'Tunnel Visionaries' on the album 'Jonah's Ark', Skyclad (1993) Noise Records (Lyrics by Martin Walkyier)

currency moved from the Gold standard to become a fiat currency. The medium became the mess it is in 1971.[8]

The book then continues with a detailed look at how Islamic Finance works. It traces its religious roots and the development, by the different schools of Islamic legal thought, of what is the only fully-worked out (although some disagreements exist) financial system backed up by religious conviction and goes on to describe the elements that make up the developing system. These elements cover a range of topics from basic sales of goods, acceptable negotiation and contracts right through to mortgages and even government project funding through the use of Sukuk.

Some of the chapters are more detailed than others and I have commented more on some aspects than others, especially where it's clear that one of authors I'm using as a professional source seems to overstate the potential beneficial impacts of adopting a financial system that is Shari'ah-based. There are ideological blinkers on both sides.

Questions

In the course of the book I will attempt to address the questions asked below.

1.   Would the current economic crisis have occurred if the world had been using IF?

2.   Would it have been possible for the rapid growth in the world economy (or even that of Europe after WW2) without the use of interest?

3.   Would not charging interest be a hindrance or a help in a modern global economy?

4.   Does an IF system have any advantages that are not found in the current, diverse, global financial system?

5.   Does an IF system have any disadvantages that are not found in the current, diverse, global financial system?

6.   Is the elimination of paying interest the most effective way to achieve or ensure social justice?

7.   Would governments be able to finance large projects over many years in a interest-free environment?

8.   Is there an ethical argument that would push people to adopt, if not all of the elements of IF, then at least some of the 'good' ideas that it proposes.

9.   What if we didn't call the ideas Islamic Finance?

---

[8] Apologies to Marshal McLuhan and those who know nothing of his work

PART ONE – An Overview of Finance

This is a brief overview of the development of finance from prehistory that ends with the current financial crisis and its sequelae. It is necessarily brief and undoubtedly idiosyncratic.

Money as a Medium of Exchange

A Creation Story

The scientific story of the creation of our Universe, supported, as always, by evidence and a working theory that allows testable predictions to be made, came into being around 13.5 billion years ago. It is called the Big Bang. In the beginning it was all just energy and the temperature was so high that not even the components that make up atoms were able to exist. It has been expanding and cooling down ever since. The Universe is nothing more than energy, some of it 'frozen out' into matter. Some tiny fraction of that matter is living. Living organisms spend their lives either as prey or predator, as energy source or energy seeker. Any movement or interaction transforms energy and contributes to the many pathways through which the Universe is cooling. In effect, energy is exchanged between living organisms with each organism trying to get as much from the exchange as possible. These exchanges are the driving power behind evolution as different patterns of genes struggle to be copied from one generation to the next. Any pattern that is more energy-efficient will stand a better chance of making it through the contingent sieve of the local environment to the next generation. The more you can get for your exchange of energy the better off you will be.

As life evolved some of these gene patterns evolved the capacity permitted to store of energy (as fat, for example) and even transfer energy. This happens when a mother suckles her young, a process in which she is donating energy in the form of food. Among these gene patterns were those that evolved into modern humans. At some point, humans developed the ability not only to collect energy as hunter-gatherers but also learned the value of storing unused energy, either as food or as items of value due to their use in the game of surviving in an environment that included both non-living and living threats; some of those threats from members of their own species.

This version, the scientific one based on masses of evidence and accepted as the basis for all biological sciences, is also accepted by the greater part of those following the Christian faith, although it's having a hard time in some parts of the USA and in certain Islamic states.

The Islamic view "holds that mainstream scientific analysis of the origin of the Universe is supported by the Quran"[9], although it's not clear what this means in reality. It is clear that, as with Christian fundamentalists in the USA, a fundamentalist resurgence in some quarters of Islamic thought is underway.

If you understand and accept this story of energy exchange as the driving power in evolution, then the question, 'What is money?' should be easy to answer as should the question 'Why do we trade?'

---

[9] "Creationism: Science and Faith in Schools" (2004), Papineau David, Guardian

Early Trade

If we say that trade is the exchange of goods between people (and I use 'if' because there is no precise scholarly definition) then trade goes back a long time in history. Starting in the Early to Middle Palaeolithic (Stone) Ages (which range from about 50,000 years to 10,000 years ago in Europe) these exchanges were carried out between individuals or small social groups, perhaps belonging to the same tribe or between kin. The exchanges comprised one or more objects or artefacts given for one or more other objects or artefacts received and they would be carried out directly between the individuals possessing the items. This type of trade, called bartering, was entirely suitable while tribal groups were generally nomadic, that is, moving around to keep in phase with the changing seasons, the migratory animals they hunted and the plants that they gathered to eat and use. The purpose of the trade was not the accumulation of resources but the transfer of resources to where they could be useful.

As the Upper Palaeolithic progressed, trade, as shown by archaeological research, became more sophisticated with evidence that objects were traded that had been created solely for that purpose and not just for day-to-day survival. An excellent example is well-documented trade in the shells of *Spondylus gaederopus*, which is a bivalve mollusc of Mediterranean origin.[10] These shells were used, "...to make various objects, especially ornaments. *Spondylus* shells (either as raw materials or as finished products) were transported far inland and are one of the most spectacular indicators of large-scale trade in Neolithic Europe".[11]

With the development of agriculture and the domestication of certain animals, the number of humans using the hunting and gathering lifestyle diminished (but has never entirely disappeared). The decrease in mobility attended the development of agricultural techniques that allowed human beings to settle and from that point the higher 'efficiency' of the city and civic life, with it concomitant focusing of power in the hands of fewer individuals, drove human history along one of the many possible paths it could have taken to where it is today.

City-based Economies

With the creation of cities and small states came the specialisation of people into trades and the need for control of resources to ensure the city or state has what it needs when resources become scarce through natural or man-made actions. Throughout this transformation of human civilisation trade has had two roles, neither of which, one could argue, was an intended one. The first was to reduce fear of 'those who speak strangely' as trading necessarily meant going out to see what could be bought and sold and from whom. The second was to provide a surplus of resources that would allow raiding missions and even warfare to be prosecuted in order to increase access to

---

[10] Séferaidès 1995 p 238
[11] Dogan and Michailidou, 2008 p22

even further resources. With the development of larger kingdoms and the amount of physical work required to maintain them, came a necessary consequence: human beings became tradable resources.

The Value of a Human Life

If you've ever wondered how much a human life is worth, then you need only read the accounts of traders, city officials and accountants from these times. In the classical literature, the following quote from Homer's Iliad is a straightforward example which, of course should not be taken too literally:

> On the day when you took me captive in the well-ordered
> orchard, and led me far from father and from friends, and sold
> me into sacred Lemnos, and I fetched you the price of one
> hundred oxen[12]

The speaker here is Lycaon, son of Priam, addressing himself to Achilles. The question remains open as to whether Achilles accepted the one hundred oxen (which were used to measure the **price** to be paid) or took other items that were also equivalent to the price of one hundred oxen. It is here that we can see the early roots of money – something of value used to put a price on something else of value, without necessarily being the something of value that is actually traded. The oxen here, it appears, were acting solely as a **marker of value** for this particular trade although it cannot be denied that the oxen themselves have an inherent value as pack animals, as food or as genetic stock.

Clearly, here is the other side of what money is. Not only can we view it as an exchange of energy but also as a marker of value (how much energy is to be exchanged).

This is not a detailed history or even a true history of how money actually came about but I trust it helps to make a point. Money is a marker that allows people on different sides of a trade to come to an agreement about the value of that trade. Instead of handing over packs of oxen, traders could hand over packs of money.

Geopolitics in One Sentence

This creates a new problem. If the money just represents value, where and when is that value created? The traders of our described past have to be able to trust that they can redeem their 'representation' of value against real oxen, if and when needed, sometime in the future. If someone, as happens nowadays, some entity can just create coins to represent value then where did the value come from to do that? What is the value of money that can be created out of thin air? The creation and distribution of money became a closely-guarded function of the state exactly for this reason. If the state cannot defeat its 'enemies' with physical force it could certainly try to drain them of resources and energy. To get to the point where you could, as a state, be drained of energy, all you would have to do would be to use a

---

[12] Homer, Iliad 21, 77-79, The Loeb Classical Library

currency issued by a more powerful state (which, of course controlled the currency) and then agree to denominate the world's most important (energy-rich) resources in that currency. This is geopolitics written in one sentence.

For a more detailed history of money, with slightly different emphases, you can consult many books, for example, 'The History of Money' by Jack Weatherford[13] or the 'Ascent of Money' by Niall Ferguson[14]

Of course it's not as bad as that, our global civilisation was made possible, not only through movement of markers of value but also by the use of representations of the movement of markers of value (such as notes, bills, IOUs and cheques). It is, however, the confusion resulting from these layers of redirection that lies at the heart of the current financial crisis, a crisis that has thrown the current system's endemic problems into high relief. The calls for a fairer, more just system will continue. Whether they are heeded or not is an entirely different matter.

Perhaps one of the options available is Islamic Finance or at least the use of ideas contained within Islamic Finance. You don't have to be a Muslim to use Islamic Finance but you would have to accept limitations on the usual way of doing things. You would not receive interest on money deposited in either a current or savings account but there would be ways to increase your money by allowing the Islamic bank to use your money in Shari'ah-compliant ways to earn money in the real economy. Also, you wouldn't pay interest on a mortgage (although you would pay a diminishing rent on the portion of your property that was owned by the bank).

---

[13] History of Money, The : Weatherford, Jack (1997) Three Rivers Press, New York
[14] Ascent of Money, The : Fergusson, Niall (2008) Penguin Books, London

A Short Historical Review of Usury

The charging and payment of interest (usury in its original formulation) is not a modern phenomenon. The idea that a borrower has to pay back more than they borrow to compensate the lender extends back, in written records, over 2,500 years.

IGIBI Bank

The IGIBI bank in Babylonia has been compared to the Rothschild's bank of the 19th century Europe. In his book, "The Evolution of Culture: The Development of Civilization to the Fall of Rome", Leslie White explains that:

> "The temples of Babylon also functioned as banks. The Igibi bank 575 BC, 'acted as buying agent for clients, loaned on crops, attaching them in advance; loaned on signatures and on objects deposited, and received deposits on which it paid interest.' The 'oldest decipherable documents from Mesopotamia are...the accounts of the temple revenues kept by the priests.' The contract as a legal device for business transactions was invented by Sumerian temple officials; it was used in rental of fields, houses, oxen, and boats. And the temple-bank of Babylon used negotiable instruments in its loan business: "Warad-llisch... has received from the sun-priestess Iltani, one shekel of silver by the Sun God's balance. This sum is to be used to buy sesame. At the time of the sesame-harvest, he will repay in sesame, at the current price, **to the bearer of this document**[15]...'"

There are records showing clearly the rate of interest to be paid for borrowing. White illustrates this:

> "Money owners lend out their money at interest. Rates of interest vary: The charge was 20 to 25 per cent in ancient Babylonia; 15 to 33 per cent in Sumer. Hammurabi fixed the legal rate at 20 per cent...50 per cent was not unusual in the Roman provinces"

Interest and the Major Religions

Islam is one of the three most popular (by number of adherents) monotheistic religions. Its roots trace back through Mosaic Law in the Old Testament to Abraham who is considered under Islam to be the first Muslim. In the Handbook of Islamic Banking, Mervyn Lewis notes that "Islam today is the only major religion that maintains a prohibition on usury, yet this distinctiveness was not always the case"[16]

---

[15] This is a negotiable financial instrument in the form of a bearer bond
[16] "Comparing Islamic and Christian attitudes to usury", Lewis M, Handbook of Islamic Banking (2007) Edward Elgar Publishing, Cheltenham, UK p 64

He notes that Hinduism, Judaism and Christianity have all, at some time in their history, opposed usury and that to mediaeval Christians, the taking of what is now called interest was a "sin, condemned in the strongest terms"[17]

Both usury and interest correspond to Riba, the literal meaning of which is excess over an original amount. The doctrinal position on usury in Christianity derives from three main sources:

> *First, there were the scriptures, especially the Gospels and the teachings of Jesus. Second, as the Middle Ages progressed and the Church became increasingly institutionalized, the words of Jesus were not sufficient to cover all eventualities and were supplemented, and to a large degree supplanted, by canon law based on the rulings of ecumenical councils and Church courts. Third, schoolmen and theologians laid the foundations of Christian theology, drawing on ethical principles developed by Greek philosophers such as Plato and Aristotle.[18]*

Biblical References to Usury

There are 4 references to usury in the Old Testament; three are in the Pentateuch and one in Psalms:

> **If thou lend money to any of my people that is poor by thee, thou shalt not be to him as a usurer, neither shall thou lay upon him usury. (Exodus 22: 25).**

> **And if thy brother be waxen poor, and fallen in decay with thee; then thou shalt relieve him: yea, though he be a stranger, or a sojourner: that he may live with thee. Take thou no usury of him, or increase: but fear thy God; that thy brother may live with thee. Thou shalt not give him thy money upon usury, nor lend him thy victuals for increase. (Leviticus 25: 35–7)**

> **Thou shalt not lend upon usury to thy brother; usury of money, usury of victuals, usury of anything that is lent upon usury: Unto a stranger thou mayest lend upon usury; but unto thy brother thou shalt not lend upon usury. (Deuteronomy 23: 19–20)**

> **Lord, who shall abide in thy tabernacle, who shall dwell in thy holy hill? He that putteth not out his money to usury, nor taketh reward against the innocent. He that doeth these things shall never be moved. (Psalm 15: 1,5)**

HH Cohn, in an entry in Encyclopaedia Judaica[19] notes that different terms for interest that appear in Leviticus and Deuteronomy, neshekh and tarbit (marbit) appear to prohibit, "…all, even minimal, interest"[20]

---

[17] *idem*

[18] *idem*

[19] 'Usury' in Encyclopaedia Judaica (1971), Jerusalem, Keter Publishing House, pp17-33

[20] *ibid* p 65

It is important to note that the quotes from the Pentateuch:

> *"...make clear that the prohibition refers to loans to 'brothers', that is, fellow members of the tribe or adherents to the common faith. Charging interest to 'foreigners' was acceptable. In this way, the Jews justified taking interest from Gentiles, and Christians charged interest to 'Saracens' (as Arabs and, by extension, Muslims in general were called in the Middle Ages)[21]*

The parable of the talents appears in both Luke and Matthew and appears to **condone** usury in the strongest possible terms. The servant who did nothing with the talents he was given is condemned to a place where there will be, "...weeping and gnashing of teeth" while his money is given to the servant who made the most.

> *Jesus told of three stewards. A rich man puts them in charge of his money. Then he leaves town. On his return, he requires an accounting. One steward had multiplied his five talents by two to one. The second had multiplied his two talents by two to one. The third had buried his coin in the ground, which he returned to the owner. Here was the response of the owner, who is symbolic of God on judgment day.*

> **Thou oughtest[22] therefore to have put my money to the exchangers, and then at my coming I should have received mine own with usury. Take therefore the talent from him, and give it unto him which hath ten talents. For unto every one that hath shall be given, and he shall have abundance: but from him that hath not shall be taken away even that which he hath. And cast ye the unprofitable servant into outer darkness: there shall be weeping and gnashing of teeth (Matthew 25:27-30).**

Roman Catholic Canon Law

Lewis summarizes the RC church position noting that:

> *The early Roman Church first condemned usury by the 44th of the Apostolic Canons at the Council of Arles in 314 followed by Nicea in 325 and Laodicia in 372. The first Canon law ruling against usury was the Papal Encyclical **Nec hoc quoque** of Saint Leo the Great, pope from 440 to 461. The last Papal Encyclical against usury, **Vix pervenit**, was issued in 1745 by Pope Benedict XIV (although it was not an infallible decree). In between, the Catholic Church maintained its opposition to the practice, although the emphasis did change over time[23]*

The initial prohibition on usury was placed on the clergy because as Roll argues, "in the absence of a developed money economy and capital market,

---

[21] *idem*

[22] This translates from Old English as '...should, therefore, have put'.

[23] Lewis *ibid* p 66

with most feudal dues rendered in kind, the Church was not only the largest production unit but also virtually the only recipient of large sums of money"[24] . As trade and commerce expanded in the later Middle Ages, the Church extended its prohibition to layman in increasingly stringent and strident forms. These condemnations came…

> …*from the great Lateran Councils, Lyon II and Vienne. The Second Lateran Council (1139) condemned usury as 'ignominious'. Lateran III (1179) introduced excommunication (exclusion from the Christian community) for open usurers. Lateran IV (1215) censured Christians who associated with Jewish usurers. Lyon II (1274) extended the condemnations to foreign usurers. Finally, the Council of Vienne (1311) allowed excommunication of princes, legislators and public authorities who either utilized or protected usurers, or who sought to distinguish between allowable interest and usury.*[25]

The Scholastics

The mediaeval schoolmen, particularly Saint Thomas Aquinas, provided the third influence on the Church's view on usury. Aquinas,

> …*succeeded in persuading the Church fathers that Aristotle's views should form the basis of Christian philosophy, and that the Arab philosophers, especially Ibn Rushd (1126–98) the Spanish–Arabian and his Christian followers, the Averroists, had misinterpreted Aristotle when developing their views on immortality. Consequently, St Thomas's Summa Theologica sought to undo this close adherence to Arabian doctrines.*

To achieve this, Aquinas emphasised Aristotle's view on usury in which he emphasised the difference between natural and unnatural modes of production. Unnatural modes, included income from lending money, violate natural law, a position that Aquinas and the Church accepted. The Scholastics offered at least ten reasons for the prohibition of usury:

- Usury contravened the teachings of Jesus
- Hebrew Law prohibited usury unambiguously
- Scriptures severely restricted loan-related activities
- Usury is contrary to the teachings of Aristotle
- Aquinas' condemned usury and added Aristotle's case with Roman Law
- Usury violates natural justice
- Usury causes inequality, which is against natural justice
- Interest was unearned income gained without work
- Usury is payment for time (time is a divine possession)
- Interest is fixed and certain (with no risk to the lender)

The views here are similar to the Islamic view. Christian attitudes expressed above see, "usury as the worst form of gain, as lacking any scriptural warrant

---

[24] *idem*
[25] *idem*

whatsoever, as involving unjustified collateral, forcing the debtor to sin, as unnatural and barren, as an unwarranted expropriation of property, as devoid of true work, and fixed, certain and lacking in risk sharing, are echoed in (or echo) Islamic views"[26]

Lewis goes on to quote al-Qaradawi's[27] four reasons for the Islamic prohibition on interest:

- Taking interest implies taking another person's property without giving him anything in exchange. The lender receives something for nothing.
- Dependence on interest discourages people from working to earn money. Money lent at interest will not be used in industry, trade or commerce, all of which need capital, thus depriving society of benefits.
- Permitting the taking of interest discourages people from doing good. If interest is prohibited people will lend to each other with goodwill expecting nothing more back than they have loaned.
- The lender is likely to be wealthy and the borrower poor. The poor will be exploited by the wealthy through the charging of interest on loans.

The Quranic View - Riba is Clearly Prohibited

Apart from the fact that the Church no longer maintains its prohibition on interest, the Quran is clearer than the Bible on the subject. In Sura 2:275 we find:

> Those who consume interest cannot stand [on the Day of Resurrection] except as one stands that is being beaten by Satan into insanity. That is because they say, "Trade is [just] like interest." But Allah has permitted trade and has forbidden interest. So whoever has received an admonition from his Lord and desists may have what is past, and his affair rests with Allah. But whoever returns to [dealing in interest or usury] - those are the companions of the Fire; they will abide eternally therein.[28]

The payment of interest for the use of borrowed money is endemic in the Western capital system and the debate for and against interest has been taking place for centuries. Despite the Roman Catholic Church issuing bulls and encyclicals clearly prohibiting usury it found itself unable to control the merchants as they expanded trade routes. These routes included trade with Muslims, who controlled large parts of the Mediterranean basin. There was also increasing trade with the Far-East, India and China. Merchants were willing to lend capital at interest for these adventures and, just as important,

---

[26] Lewis *ibid* pp 69-70

[27] *ibid* p 70

[28] Sura 2 (275) This is from an online version of the Koran at http://quran.com/2 accessed 14 Mar 2013

people were **willing to pay the interest** for the chance to become successful traders.

The mercantile position changed little through the years. In England, several laws were passed on the rates that could be charged but total prohibition never took hold. The debate continued into the 17th and 18th centuries with further interesting contributions made by Bentham[29], Thornton[30] and Smith[31] and Keynes[32].

In general, the contributions arguing against the charging of interest were that:

- Interest discourages the spirit of enterprise because, immediately following the loan, without having made a return on the money, the borrower has to pay interest and reimburse capital
- Interest causes inflation
- Interest, being a charge, causes an increase in the sale price
- Interest causes a split between the real economy and the monetary economy

The charging of interest on loans and mortgages and the payment of interest for savings and current accounts is an almost invisible part of the fabric of our society in the West. Governments lend and borrow at interest, as do banks, credit unions and building societies. Pension annuities rely entirely on the concept and it is simple and quick to use. However, a Muslim is not even permitted to pay interest on a loan or mortgage. This is a position that has made life financially-challenging for Muslims living in non-Islamic states wishing to buy a house. Many have had to bow to the realpolitik of their chosen homeland or do without a house. There is now, however, the diminishing musharakah mortgage[33] to meet their needs.

---

[29] Bentham, Jeremy, Letters on Usury (1787) Letter 2 paragraph 7
"...why he [Bentham is referring to Government legislators] should set his face against the owners of that species of property [Bentham is referring to money as property] more than of any other? Why he should make it his business to prevent their getting *more* than a certain price for the use of it, rather than to prevent their getting *less?*"

[30] Thornton Henry, An Enquiry into the Nature and Effects of Paper Credit of Great Britain (1802)

[31] Smith Adam, Wealth of Nations (1776) Smith preferred to leave the markets to make the rates that would allow appropriate liquidity

[32] Keynes, J M, The General Theory of Employment, Interest and Money

[33] The diminishing musharakah-based mortgage is described in more detail in later chapters

The Global Financial System and Its Current Problems

Whatever proportion of the world economy one could reasonably expect Shari'ah-compliant finance to replace, it is important to see why the ideas behind it might be useful to have in mind. What is the basis of the current global system and why is it constantly under pressure?

Bretton Woods

The current global system of monetary management was created by agreements undertaken in July 1944 (towards the end of the Second World War) between 44 Allied countries at the Mount Washington Hotel, Bretton-Woods in the US State of New Hampshire. The Bretton Woods system was the first example of a fully negotiated monetary order intended to govern monetary relations between independent nation-states.

The agreement led to the creation of the International Monetary Fund (IMF) and the International Bank for Reconstruction and Development (which is now part of the World Bank). The main features were that each country was obligated to tie its currency to the value of the US Dollar and that the IMF would provide loans to bridge temporary imbalances in balances of payments between nations.

Nixon Ends the Gold Standard

The value of the dollar itself was tied to the value of gold and led to a period of stability in global financial affairs where it was possible to exchange dollars for physical gold at $35 per ounce and vice versa at US Treasury "gold windows". This continued until August 1971 when President Richard Nixon unilaterally terminated the convertibility of dollars into gold. He did this to redress US economic problems generated by the Vietnam War and the problem of European countries, such as West Germany and Switzerland, purchasing goods created by their recovered economies. These and other countries also exchange their reserve dollars for physical gold which was then transported to their own vaults. The "Nixon Shock" made the dollar into a fiat currency which as Paul Krugman[34] noted in 1996 causes its own problems as:

> The current world monetary system assigns no special role to gold; indeed, the Federal Reserve is not obliged to tie the dollar to anything. It can print as much or as little money as it deems appropriate. There are powerful advantages to such an unconstrained system. Above all, the Fed is free to respond to actual or threatened recessions by pumping in money. To take only one example, that flexibility is the reason the stock market crash of 1987—which started out every bit as frightening as

---

[34] Krugman is a Nobel Prize-Winning liberal economist with over 20 books and 200 scholarly articles to his name

that of 1929—did not cause a slump in the real economy. While freely floating national money has advantages, however, it also has risks. For one thing, it can create uncertainties for international traders and investors. Over the past five years, the dollar has been worth as much as 120 yen and as little as 80. The costs of this volatility are hard to measure...

Third World Debt

There are various reasons why the so-called Third World countries are had to borrow money and became indebted. Some of these debts, for example, were no more than debts incurred by their former colonial powers. This topic has received extensive attention elsewhere and, if the topic interests you, there are some resources on the web that give detailed descriptions of the issue and potential solutions. The matter of importance for this book is the problem relating to the dollar as a fiat currency while it is still the world's reserve currency. The South Centre[35] explains why, in their view, there is a problem:

> *The history of third world debt is the history of a massive siphoning-off by international finance of the resources of the most deprived peoples. This process is designed to perpetuate itself thanks to a diabolical mechanism whereby debt replicates itself on an ever greater scale, a cycle that can be broken only by canceling the debt. According to a new Working Paper on "Effects of debt on human rights" prepared by Mr. El Hadji Guissé for current UN Sub Commission on Human Rights (E/CN.4/Sub.2/2004/27), the developing countries' debt is partly the result of the unjust transfer to them of the debts of the colonizing States! A sum of US$ 59 billion external in public debt was imposed on the newly independent States in 1960. With the additional strain of an **interest rate unilaterally set at 14 per cent**, [my emphasis] this debt increased rapidly. Before they had even had time to organize their economies and get them up and running, the new debtors were already saddled with a heavy burden of debt*

Many Third World countries, unable to make interest payments on time, have had these missed payments added to the balance that has to be paid. This has the obvious consequence that the debt that they couldn't pay for already has now become even bigger. The international organizations (IMF for example) and private creditors, are willing to see the people of a country starve as these countries export food stuffs to raise cash (in dollars) in order to meet the debt repayments (in dollars) on the loans that they had no choice about taking out in the first place in a currency that wasn't even their own.

Even the oil-rich countries of the world came to suffer from the pricing of their oil resources in dollars. Unfortunately, as the US economy suffered,

---

[35] The South Centre at http://www.southcentre.org/ is an intergovernmental policy think-tank for developing countries

following the Nixon Shock, the US Treasury printed more dollars – and, by the simplest of economic principles, the value of the dollar went down. This means that the value of the oil exported by oil-rich countries went down. These countries could buy fewer foreign goods and services as the price of oil in dollars remained fixed and the value of the dollars went down. This remained the problem until OPEC raised the price of oil in 1973, sparking one of the greatest crises for the global economy.

With debt denominated in dollars, the problem of Third World debt increased. With interest payments added to increased debt balances the debts for most nations increased rather than decreased and entered a state of "unpayability" that crippled their economies and impoverished their people.

All of this is taking place while at the same time some of their so-called leaders siphoned off significant part of the loans to their own bank accounts in the West. Some of these Western banks then promptly re-lent the money to others including the country from which it had effectively been stolen and for which they now end up paying twice. The banks take their cut both ways. The system is patently unjust and abusive and the problem is magnified by the denomination of the debt in a fiat currency over which the lending country has no oversight, let alone control. Despite some debt cancellation, the problem remains significant for many Third World countries who seem destined to remain Third World.[36]

US Debt and the Future of the Dollar

As the guardian of the dollar, the US has been able to finance its spending by, among other things, creating debt (an obligation to repay borrowed money). This debt is issued mainly in the form of US Treasury securities that are backed by the US government with a promise to repay the principal borrowed from the lender at a fixed later date called the maturity. The holder of the debt is paid a constant regular premium (interest) every 6 months up until maturity. The interest payment is called the coupon.

The total US debt at the end of April 2013 was $16.83 TRILLION[37] (that's nearly $54,000 for each man, woman and child in the USA). To finance that debt, in US Fiscal Year 2012, the US Treasury paid $359,796,008,919.49 interest (Three Hundred and Fifty Nine BILLION Dollars). In the current fiscal year between October 2012 and April 2013 interest was $227,870,358,779.45 with $95,736,594,801.52 paid out in December 2012 alone[38].

There is increasing concern among other nations that this level of debt is unsustainable in the long run. The debt is never reduced – in the 12 first years of the 21st century the US debt has tripled from 5½ to more than 16½ trillion dollars. Future generations are being burdened with interest payments

---

[36] See the section "Geopolitics in One Sentence" in Chapter 3

[37] The US Treasury "Monthly Statement of the Public Debt" which can be found at: http://www.treasurydirect.gov/govt/reports/pd/mspd/2013/2013_apr.htm

[38] US Treasury "Interest on the Debt Outstanding" at http://www.treasurydirect.gov/govt/reports/ir/ir_expense.htm

that eat into the wealth of nations and that generate little of long-term value except cash for the lenders. Perhaps the most worrying is that the repayments listed above, large as they may be, **are generated when interest rates are at historical low values**. The current yields on US Treasuries are shown in the table below and represent the "market value" of US Treasuries traded in the secondary markets (the markets where US Treasuries are sold among investors after they have been issued by the Treasury Department). The figures quoted are percentages.

Maturity	1 yr	2 yr	3 yr	5 yr	7 yr	10 yr	20 yr	30 yr
2 Jan 2013	0.15	0.27	0.37	0.76	1.25	1.86	2.63	3.04

Although these rates are low, investors are still happy to buy US debt as it is considered safe debt – the likelihood of default is believed to be negligible.

Now look at what the same treasuries cost the US fifteen years ago:

Maturity	1 yr	2 yr	3 yr	5 yr	7 yr	10 yr	20 yr	30 yr
2 Jan 1998	5.46	5.59	5.62	5.63	5.68	5.67	5.94	5.86
Ratio 1998:2013	36.4	20.7	15.2	7.4	4.5	3.0	2.3	1.9

This means that fifteen years ago, the US Treasury was paying 36 times as much interest to fund its 1-year bills and 3 times as much interest to fund its 10-year notes. In January 1998, the total debt outstanding was $5.3 TRILLION. This is less than one third of its current value. As a rough figure, this suggests that the interest payments on the USA's debt could be about nine times higher if the rates returned to those of 1998!

Could the US Treasury afford to finance the debt at those rates? The point to remember is that the rates are low due to the efforts of the US Federal Reserve to get the banks to borrow money so that, in turn, they can use it to lend on to small businesses and industry to get the economy started again. If this cheap money triggers inflation or institutional or other lenders start demanding a greater return on Treasuries (because they can get a better return elsewhere, then the Treasury will have to respond by paying increased rates for new and rolled-over US debt. This is certainly a significant problem for the dollar and, because the dollar is the world's reserve currency, a problem for the global financial system. The potential outcomes no doubt form the core of models at central banks, the IMF and World Bank but what will happen and when and the consequences of this do not form part of the ongoing public debate.

Black-Scholes

The mathematical model including the Black-Scholes equation was published in 1973. One of its authors (Myron Scholes) and a fellow researcher (Robert Merton) were awarded the Nobel Prize for Economics in 1997. Fischer Black died before the prize was awarded and was, therefore, ineligible to receive the prize. The equation was derived, says Ian Stewart, to provide "a rational way to price a financial contract when it still had time to run"[39]

It worked while as it was used within the parameters that it was derived to model. However, as the market in the newly-created 'products' called derivatives (developed as a result of the equation) proved so successful, the financial institutions and the traders who used the equation forgot about, ignored or were unaware of the conditions under which the equation could be safely used. The equation lost its context and the global financial system lost its stability as a result.

The main limitation was that the value of the underlying assets should not be subject to any significant change in value. As the value of mortgages[40] based on sub-primes equity plunged in 2006/7, the Black-Scholes equation tore the heart out of the market in these opaque derivatives. This market had somehow reached a value that exceeded ten times all of the wealth generated by the global economy in the previous 100 years! The Black-Scholes equation, used in circumstances where it should not have been became a black hole with the global financial system spiralling in on itself. The ringdown from the coalescence will continue to disturb the system for years to come. One could easily blame the Black-Scholes equation but, "the equation was just one ingredient in a rich stew of financial irresponsibility, political ineptitude, perverse incentives and lax regulation".[41]

Interestingly, Stewart then goes on to argue that the system "desperately needs a radical overhaul and that requires more mathematics, not less…" But then, he is a Professor of Mathematics. Perhaps what the system need is less mathematics. Finance should be easy to understand, more people should be clear about what is happening to their personal money and to their pensions. The system needs a radical overhaul but I suspect it will get a minor tweak.

Robert Peston, the BBC's Business editor, has written a clear book[42] on what he perceives the problems to be. The financiers and traders have turned away completely from supporting useful socially productive projects towards trying to make quick profits using complex instruments operating outside their design parameters. Peston notes that German investment in manufacturing is 12 times that of the UK. It is clear to most observers that the German economy is all the better for it.

---

[39] "The mathematical equation that caused the banks to crash" Stewart Ian, (2012) Guardian
[40] These were the underlying real-world assets on which the derivative contracts were based.
[41] Stewart *ibid*
[42] How Do We Fix This Mess? Peston, Robert (2013), Hodder and Staunton, London

PART TWO – Introduction to Islam and Islamic Finance

A Short Introduction to Islam

Bis-mi-Allah-e-Rahman-e-Rahim

"We begin in the name of God, the compassionate and the merciful".

To appreciate Islamic Finance you need to be aware of the main elements of Islam. This short chapter covers the early history of Islam from the 7th to the 12th centuries CE. For this chapter, I have drawn inspiration from the book, 'Islam' by Azra Kidwai which, although it is written in English, I found in a dusty corner of an old bookshop here in Brussels.

A Brief History

Byzantine and Sassanian Empires

In the late 6th and early 7th century, the Byzantine and Sassanian Empires converged to the north of the Arabian Peninsula, which in earlier times had been the border between the Egyptian and Mesopotamian civilisations, both irrigated by the Nile and the Tigris respectively. Arabia had no rivers, no cultivation and the prosperity of the nearby empires passed by while the Sun beat down mercilessly on the rocks and sand inhabited by hardy nomadic tribes reliant on limited water, food and their pack animal, the camel.

The Byzantine and Sassanian empires used a close relationship between church and state. The Byzantine Empire was Christian while in the Sassanian Empire Zoroastrianism had a widespread influence. Both of these empires had vast (dare one say, Byzantine) bureaucracies, large areas of fertile land, large armies and busy trade routes. Both Christianity and Zoroastrianism were monotheistic in nature; they believed in the prophetic tradition, a universal scripture and one transcendental god. They also believed in one life on Earth and after death, the choice between Heaven and Hell was dependent on one's actions during your life. This was significant in the early growth of Islam.

Surviving on the Arabian Peninsula

The Arabian Peninsula was effectively barren and it was not worth the salt fighting off tribesman for no gain in material resources. The tribes were called Bedouins and each tribe was made up of several clans claiming common ancestry. Some of the tribes had settled in the rare areas where water could be found and a bare minimum of resources cultivated. Other tribes continued their nomadic existence constantly moving round in search of food and water. The lack of significant resources led, of course, to fights over the resources and a constant tension between tribes trying to gain the upper hand. This difficult existence was not made any simpler by the tradition of blood feud – every death of a tribe member had to be avenged in blood. The inevitable cycle of violence made trade, if it was at all imaginable, almost impossible.

The tribes were, however, linked by a common language, a rich literary tradition and belief in, "a vague figure called Allah, the supreme god regarded as the Creator."[43]

As tribes were small, there were no rich or poor, all were equal. When all you can possess is what you can carry with you, the acquisition of wealth is not a significant motivator. "Tribal values were based on hereditary economic and social solidarity expressed through shared responsibilities and resources in good times and bad"[44]. The tribe was made up of clans that were in turn made up from families. They were led by a selected (not hereditary) leader called a Saiyyid whose decisions were binding and they rejected authoritarian forms of government. This was also significant in the early growth of Islam.

Trade across the Peninsula

The constant warfare between the Byzantine and Sassanian Empires eventually meant that the Bedouins became crucial to trade. The blocked routes to the north meant alternative routes across the Peninsula had to be found and as a result:

> ...textiles, spices and luxury foods from the East were brought by sea to the southern ports of the Peninsula. From ports in Yemen they were transported over land on camel-back to the Mediterranean ports. Similarly, goods from Africa, particularly slaves - who were in great demand – were shipped across the Red Sea and then conveyed over land to markets in Asia. Commerce and trading thus exposed the Arabs to the workings of big empires and the intricacies of world trade.[45]

Mecca

At the crossroads of the trade routes a small city sitting on a spring houses the Ka'ba, the shrine most important to the Bedouin tribes. Each year a pilgrimage of tribespeople to the shrine was accompanied by a fair that brought in good business. This was vital to the city's economy and survival, which was entirely dependent on imported food and goods.

The trade routes passing through Mecca meant that the Bedouin who settled there became adept in the complexities of international trade while becoming successful traders in their own right. The city was controlled by one of the largest of the Bedouin tribes in Arabia, the Quraysh. The tribe successfully negotiated with other tribes, organizing the trade system to their own advantage. Some estimates of trade with Syria alone indicate annual trade amounted to the equivalent of eleven thousand kilograms of gold.[46]

---

[43] Kidwai (2004) p 10
[44] idem
[45] Kidwai op cit p 12
[46] At today's prices, this represents about €350,000,000 per annum

The Quraysh accommodated the gods of other tribes within the Ka'ba[47] shrine and the safety of all those who came during the annual pilgrimage called the Hajj. They also ensured that no warfare was conducted during the four months of the year that they deemed to be sacred. The ensuing peace was an important factor in the flourishing of trade.

Muhammed

Muhammed was born into the Banu Hashim clan of the Quraysh tribe in 570 CE. He was raised by his grandfather and then later by his uncle. He became a successful trader and married a women fifteen years his senior at the age of 25. His wife, Khadija, also became his friend and supported him through his initial spiritual struggles. He was visited by the archangel Gabriel during one of his regular visits to meditate in the local mountains. Khadija believed fervently that her husband's visitation was not a dream and that God had chosen Muhammed to renew the people's faith. Muhammed recognized himself as Rasul Allah (Messenger of God) and continued to receive these messages until his death.

The Message

The message was one of:

> ...divine and sublime beauty [and] was a warning to the heedless, a guide to the erring, an assurance to those in doubt and solace to those suffering[48]

Muhammed's message from God stressed an obligation to the poor and the destitute and warned those who hoarded wealth and exploited the helpless of the impending day of judgement. He emphasised a community based on a common faith (not clan or tribal ties) and the equality of all before their creator in a society where economic and social separation and inequality had become entrenched. Individuals had, he said, the freedom to act but that they had to be responsible for their own actions.

His message was popular with the members of weaker clans and junior members of powerful clans as well as tribal clients and slaves. His message was not, however, popular with those in control of Mecca who became alarmed when well-to-do Meccans converted to the new religion. Muhammed's clan ties protected him until Abu Talib, the leader of his clan died in 619 CE and the new clan chief, worried about economic boycott, withdrew his support. Without clan protection Muhammed and his Muslims migrated from Mecca on 24 September 622 CE. The journey to Yathrib (Medina), 280 kilometres north of Mecca, is called the hijra and marks the breaking away from the old clan ties. Muslims, irrespective of clan, tribe or race, were now free to form a community, called the ummah, under God. The hijra, the lunar-based Muslim calendar, starts from this day.

---

[47] The Ka'ba, it is believed, was built on God's orders by Abraham. One of Abraham's sons, Ismail is the ancestor of Muhammed, the other son, Isaac, is the ancestor of the Jews. This means that all three monotheistic religions descend from the Abrahamic tradition
[48] Kidwai op cit p 14

Medina

The small agricultural community at Medina welcomed Muhammed and his followers. Muhammed, whose reputation as a wise man had preceded him, was invited to act as mediator (hakam) in the small but bloody disputes that were prevalent at the time. He made converts to the new faith while making a formal agreement between Muhammed and the people of Medina. The document survives to this day as the Constitution of Medina and called for one community made up from three groups: the emigrants (muhajirun), the hosts at Medina (ansars) and the Jews as a protected religious group.

From Medina, Muhammed challenged the Meccan trading system by harassing caravans *en route* between Mecca and Syria and within two years the Muslims had gained a large amount of money, four-fifths of which was distributed among all the Muslims, with one-fifth being used to manage and pay for the affairs of the community.

With the challenge to peninsular trade, conflict with Mecca became unavoidable but it was soon realised that for any kind of prosperity to arise, peace would have to be made. Muhammed announced his intention to perform the Hajj to the shrine at Mecca. In 630 CE a truce was arranged whereby the Muslims were allowed to enter the city of Mecca with the agreement that it was not to be taken as spoils of war. Muhammed made it clear that Islam held the shrine in the highest esteem and performed many pre-Islamic rituals while on his pilgrimage.

Following the taking of Mecca, Muhammed became the supreme political and religious authority within the ummah. Most of the unconverted Medinans became Muslim on Muhammed's return with the remaining Jews and Christians given the status of zimmis or protected people. The reduced amount of intertribal fighting meant that the Muslims now needed to look elsewhere for sources of income. During the final years of his life Muhammed focused on securing trade routes with Iraq and Syria. This continued until his death in 624 CE when he died in the chamber of his favourite wife, Ayesha. His grave is now part of the mosque complex, called Masjid-e-Nabi, that has been built at that spot.

The Caliphs

The first four successors to Muhammed were called the Khalifat ar Rasul or Viceroys of the Messenger. They came from among the Companions of the Prophet and were called the 'Rightly Guided Caliphs'.

Abu Bakr

The first Caliph was Abu Bakr who spent most of his short time in the role (632-634 CE) establishing the political and religious authority of Medina over the Arabian Peninsula and defeating the Byzantine and Sassanian Empires so that Islam was able to expand beyond the Peninsula.

Umar

The second caliph, Umar (634-644 CE) expanded the influence of Islam taking control of Damascus, Ctesiphon[49], Jerusalem, Alexandria and Mosul. Egypt and Iran were now under Muslim rule. Umar was an excellent administrator and his rule laid the foundations for the institutions of an Islamic regime. On taking control, all legal, economic and social structures were left in place but the rulers were replaced.

Only movable wealth gained as battle booty and taxes were collected by the new regime. Four-fifths of the wealth was then distributed among the Islamic community. Peoples in conquered areas did not have to convert. Non-Muslims were given the status of zimmis and had to pay a land tax and a tax on each adult individual called the jaziya.

Usman

The next Caliph, Usman, was elected by a council and he continued the expansion further into Iran and Egypt. Usman, however, did come under criticism for his choice of governors which resulted in power being concentrated in one family. His choice of Muawiyyah, one of his cousins, as governor of Syria was certainly controversial and would have a significant impact later.

Qurra and the Standardisation of the Quran

God's revelations to Muhammed were memorised by many of his early followers, some of it had even been written down on the shoulder blades of camels and pieces of papyrus. The Qurra were the people who recited the Quran from memory and were held in great esteem as people's only access to the words of God in the Quran. Umar ordered the standardisation of the Quran and suppressed all versions but the standardized one leading to outrage and protest among those Qurra whose renderings were excluded.

Civil War and Shi'at ul Ali

Ali had been one of the first converts to Islam and was considered brave, pious and idealistic. After Usman was murdered by discontented Muslims from Kufah in 656 Ali took the opportunity to declare himself Caliph; a position he held for six years from 656 CE moving, for military reasons, the capital from Medina to Kufah. The resulting civil war resulted in the deaths of many including those who had been Companions of the Prophet. As his support grew a group among them came to be known as the Shi'at ul Ali (the party of Ali) or Shias.

The Umayyads

Muawiyyah restarted the expansion of the ummah, moving into eastern Iran and over into the Oxus valley. He conquered Africa as far as Algeria.

---

[49] Ctesiphon was one of the great cities of late ancient Mesopotamia becoming prominent in the first century BCE. The ruins of the city are located on the east bank of the Tigris in Baghdad Governorate, Iraq, approximately 35 km south of the city of Baghdad

However, his nomination of his son, Yazid, caused the Shias to set up their own regime at Kufah. The slaughter of Husayn with his three sons (Ali Asghar, Ali Akbar and Abbas) and the public display of the severed head of Husayn by Muawiyyah's son, Yazid, had a traumatic effect on the Muslim community. The resistance to Yazid became widespread and the next Caliph, Yazid's son, Abdal Malik (685-705 CE),

> ...crushed the Medinan resistance and in the process of re-establishing the authority of the Caliph, the Ka'ba was damaged. Abdal Malik's efforts to maintain the political unity of the Muslims was accompanied by state investment in irrigation and economic development. A uniform way of reciting the Quran was imposed and judges (qazis) were appointed in various garrison towns to settle disputes among Muslims.[50]

The invasion of Spain started in 711 CE and the entire peninsula had fallen in a little over two years. Spain was given the name Andalusia by the Arabs and an amalgam of Arabic, Spanish and Berber elements produced the Moorish culture. At the same time, the caliph's armies pushed in Sindh and in central Asia the caliphate ended up sharing boundaries with China. To support this expansion, administrative unity was ensured using centrally-appointed governors. The success of the caliph relied on direct control over economic resources; they abolished tax privileges for former elites and brought in equitable tax systems which were welcomed by the common people. They ensured further support by removing religious discrimination and refusing to interfere in the religious affairs of conquered territories.

The Abbasids

A cousin of the Prophet called Abu'l Abbas, supported by the Shias, challenged the Umayyads successfully. The first Abbasid Caliph was proclaimed in 750 CE.

The Abbasid victory marks the beginning of the end of Syrian dominance over the affairs of the Caliphate. The Abbasids were successful because they supported more popular causes, inducting new groups into the ruling elite and then holding this heterogeneous new elite together by developing a court-generated 'high-culture'.

They became patrons of Islamic learning, reducing the criticism of antagonistic religious groups. They involved the learned Muslims of the ulama in formulating and then disseminating cultural and religious tradition that applied to all Muslims. The Abbasids did, however, impose an absolutist state structure, adopting court structure of the Sassanians and projecting themselves as semi-divine individuals with titles such as 'Shadow of God on Earth'. Courtiers were required to kiss the ground in front of the Caliphs who gave themselves the right to dispense summary and unchallengeable justice.

---

[50] idem

Opposition was dealt with severely. An elaborate bureaucracy and an effective espionage system strengthened their hold over the empire. Financial matters were entrusted to a trustworthy noble. This responsibility was to evolve into the permanent office of the wazir, the all-powerful minister of subsequent Muslim empires.[51]

Harun al Rashid

The best-known of the Abbasid caliphs, Harun al Rashid (785-809 CE), was based in Baghdad and,

...ran an efficient state managed by trained bureaucrats [and] encouraged artists, poets and musicians and rewarded them liberally. The aristocracy followed his example and Baghdad soon became a flourishing cultural and intellectual centre. Sciences and metaphysics were studied, the technique of paper-making was imported from China and soon paper replaced papyrus. Books on astronomy, medicine and mathematics were translated into Arabic from Greek and Sanskrit[52]

The economy grew as a result of the comparative peace and enormous size of the empire and,

Banking, credit and postal services developed, towns increasingly became the hub of intense commercial activity. One indirect result of the economic developments in the history of Islam was that the religion won new adherents. Many who flocked to the towns found it convenient to convert. This led to the development of a more populist form of Islam in which the new converts carried their old traditions. This Islam was free from theological debates and was more of a way of life than a dogma.[53]

The splendour and grandeur of al Rasid's reign has led many to believe that Baghdad provides the background for the Arabian Nights. Unfortunately, his decision to split the empire among his three sons on his death led to a civil war. Many governors of distant territories started assuming autonomous roles and the next few centuries saw a crumbling caliphate splitting into independent kingdoms. In Tunisia, the Aghlabids were followed by the Fatimids who also controlled Egypt. In Yemen, the Zaydi Shias took control while Hamdanis did in Mosul. In north-eastern Iran, it was the Samanids.

The Muslims were now one ummah living in different states and in each state Islam developed slightly differently. However, the developments were never isolated as contact between Muslims was maintained with strong cultural links.

---

[51] Kidwai *op cit* p 34
[52] *op cit* p 35
[53] *idem*

Beliefs and Duties

Reading the Quran

Islam means submission to the will of Allah: The One and Only God who is the Compassionate and the Merciful.

God's guidance has been,

> ...revealed through various prophets, like Moses and Jesus, each of whom is identified with a revealed book (the Torah and the Gospel). Muhammed is considered the last and greatest of all the Prophets; and his Quran supersedes all previous books of revelation and is considered [by Muslims] to be the final word of God[54]

That the Quran was sent by God is revealed by God himself in Sura 2:2 of the Quran:

> **Mankind was one single nation**
> **And God sent Messengers**
> **With glad tidings and warnings**
> **And with them He sent**
> **The Book in truth**
> **To judge between people**
> **In matters wherein they differed**
> **God by His Grace**
> **Guided the Believers**
> **To the Truth,**
> **Concerning that wherein they differed**
> **For God guides**
> **Whom He will**
> **To a path**
> **That is straight**

Muhammed recited the words of God to his growing audience. His words were compiled into the Quran after his death.

The word Quran means recitation or reading and it a facsimile of the word of God inscribed on a tablet in Heaven. It comprises 114 chapters called suras arranged in order of length with each sura made up from a number of ayats – the actual units of the Quran. The book is divided into 30 equal parts (called juz in Arabic). Reading the Quran is a duty of every Muslim and is one way of worshipping God. Through this act one can affirm one's faith and arrive, in the end, at the knowledge of God. The message is written in beautiful, lyrical Arabic that is difficult to convey in any translation. Within the Quran,

> ...simple analogies and well-known historical references are used to emphasize God's unity.[55]

---

[54] Kidmai *op cit* p 41

[55] Kidmai *op cit* p 42

The Quran differs from the other revealed books in the sense that it provides specific guidance on how to conduct one's life and affairs in order to please God - it is not an abstract document. It prescribes duties for Muslims and proscribes things deemed unacceptable while, at the same time, Islam acknowledges that humans have wills of their own and that they must make their own choices. It reminds them of the Day of Judgement when the good will be rewarded in Heaven and sinners will pay in Hell.

Farz – Essential Duties of a Muslim

The five pillars of the faith are:
- Faith (Kalima)
- Prayers (Salah)
- Fasting (Roza)
- Charity (Zakat)
- Pilgrimage (Hajj)

Faith

As a matter of faith a good Muslim must recite and believe the declaration that:

"There is no God but Allah and Muhammed is his Prophet". It is also believed that recitation of this declaration allows a person entry into the Muslim faith.

Prayer

Muslims confirm their belief by praying to God five times a day:
- Fajir (before sunrise)
- Zohr (early afternoon – when an object's shadow equals the object's length)
- Asr (Yellowing of the Sun)
- Maghrib (The setting of the Sun until the red of the Sun disappears)
- Isha (night prayers)

The prayers are verses of the Quran broken into units and at the end of each prayer the worshipper prostrates himself on the ground. Before praying a Muslim makes a ritual cleansing (wuzu) and during prayer he will be facing the qibla, the Ka'ba in Mecca. Prayer is usually collective but this is not compulsory. They are led by an imam or anyone who is sufficiently knowledgeable to be accepted as such. Friday afternoon prayers are compulsory at the local mosque. The call to prayer, adaan, is carried out by the muezzin.

Fasting

Fasting occurs during the Islamic month of Ramadan from the sighting of the new moon. It is forbidden to drink or eat between the hours of sunrise and sunset with the two meals (one before sunrise and one after) called sahri and iftar. It is believed that this practice inculcates the principle of austerity and helps believers understand the sufferings of the needy. Those unable to fast for unavoidable reasons such as ill health can give fixed amounts to charity. The month of Ramadan ends with the sighting of the next new moon and the celebration of Id-ul-Fitr.

Charity

Every Muslim is required to give one-fortieth of his or her possessions including cash, jewellery, animals, agricultural and other produce. The practice emphasises the responsibility of Muslims to their less fortunate brothers and sisters. Under Islam everything belongs to God and one must use God's possessions as God would by sharing them with the poor. The Quran insists that Zakat be given only to the poor and the deserving. There are priorities laid down for how this is to be done: to a deserving relative, to the disabled and to the poor in that order.

Pilgrimage

The pilgrimage to Mecca continues the tradition of the Bedouin tribes in pre-Islamic times and celebrates the return of Muhammed to Mecca after the Meccans accepted and converted to Islam. Each Muslim with the health and the wherewithal to do so must make the Hajj once in his life time. The pilgrimage is undertaken over the eighth, ninth and tenth days of the last lunar month of the year which is called Dhul i Hijja. If the pilgrimage is conducted at some other time of year it is not considered Hajj but Umra. All pilgrims are dressed alike in ihram while they worship collectively, the aim being to eliminate racial and social differences. If it is impossible for someone to travel, the Quran suggests that that person pays for the Hajj of a poor person.

Shari'ah

Guidelines for a Good Muslim

The Quran is not the only source of guidelines for a good Muslim's life. The other sources, none of which may contradict anything written in the Quran, add other essential advice. These other sources are the Sunnah, the Shari'ah and the Fiqh.

Sunnah and Hadith

These are the ways and practices of the Prophet, whose life has always been a source of inspiration for practising Muslims. Everything that the Prophet did is considered worthy of emulation and became the ideal for how to be a pious Muslim. The Sunnah was preserved after the death of the Prophet through the tradition of the Hadith. The hadith have forged a link between Muslims and their prophet. The aim was to prevent people from wrongly attributing facts to him. Witnesses and a chain of authority linking directly to the Prophet had to be provided to substantiate each Hadith before it was accepted. A sample Hadith is shown below:

"Religion is very easy and whoever overburdens himself in his religion will not be able to continue in that way. So you should not be extremists, but try to be near to perfection and receive the good tidings that you will be rewarded."[56]

Shari'ah and Fiqh

The actual rules governing 'the Way' in which Muslims lead their lives is called Shari'ah. The Shari'ah covers everything about how a Muslim leads his life from birth to the distribution of his possessions after his death. In order to develop Shari'ah it was necessary to create a science of Islamic jurisprudence. This science is called Fiqh. Fiqh itself has four roots; the Quran, the Hadith, the Ijma'a and the Qiyas. Ijma'a means consensus and it recognizes the intention of Muslims to work through commonly-accepted views on contentious issues. Qiyas is a way of finding solutions through analogy by referring to similar situations in the Hadith. Fiqh as the science of Islamic jurisprudence was development following widespread debate within the Muslim community.

The Schools (Madhab)

As with any body of knowledge, different schools of thought formed with slightly different historical traditions. The main differences are about methodology and small details and not about the core values of Islam or interpretation of the Quran. Each scholar had great respect for each of the other scholars – the schools were not in opposition. They sought the true meaning of God's words, ensuring that Shari'ah was a protection for the poor and weak members of society and that were possible laws were based in custom, so that it could be understood.

Each school of jurisprudence identifies with the revered master of each school:

- Hanafi after Abu Hanifa (702 - 767 CE)
- Maliki after Malik bin Anas (716 - 796 CE)
- Shafi'i after Al Shafi'i (767 - 820 CE)
- Hanbali after Ahmad bin Hanbal (780 – 855 CE)

Throughout the history of Islam, jurists have attached themselves to a school; each one having a slightly different interpretation in some areas of the law. This is true today in the development of the rules that are being developed to govern the emerging area of Islamic Finance and these names appear throughout the later descriptions of the structure of Islamic Finance in the modern interpretation.

---

[56] Sahih Bukhari, Volume 1, Book 2, Number 38

Western Perspective of Islam and Shari'ah

Zeitgeist – Bad Press for Islam

The mainstream narrative relating to Islam in the British media over the last 30 years is, if the response of Muslim representatives is to be believed, wrong. Although it is easy to oversimplify the argument, from a Western perspective the narrative is (as narrative always are) a selective distillation of public understandings in response to several events and ongoing themes and their media representation filtered through Western sensibilities and necessary prejudices. Here I am not using "prejudices" in any pejorative sense – we are products of our upbringing and need to understand that clearly when analysing events and formulating opinions as well as policy.

In the modern era, one event that triggered a significant reaction and set the scene for current UK attitudes was the decision (fatwa) delivered in February 1989 by the Supreme Leader of Iran, Ayatollah Khomeini against Salman Rushdie. Rushdie's fifth book published in 1988. 'The Satanic Verses', a novel recognised as a study in immigrant isolation and confusion includes some alleged Koranic verses deemed 'blasphemous to Islam'. The fatwa, calling for the death penalty against Rushdie (himself a Muslim by education), was the direct cause of public book burnings and the death of a Japanese translator of the Satanic Verses at the hands of extremists.[57] Rushdie had to go into hiding and was given police protection in the UK.

Without doubt the most dramatic associated with Muslim extremism was the destruction of the two towers of the World Trade Centre (WTC) in New York on 11 Sep 2001 (9/11/01 in US calendar notation) with the deaths of over three thousand people[58]. The ongoing effects of this event continue to impact US policy despite the death of its author, Osama bin Laden, nearly 10 years later.

Many other events can be related, for example death threats against satirical cartoonists in Denmark[59] for representations of the Prophet Mohammed. The mutual misunderstanding is obvious as people in Western democracies reinforce calls for freedom of the press and expression while at the same time there are calls from some Muslim groups demanding that the "blasphemers" be killed.

There are also frequent news reports of savage and repressive behaviour by members of the Taliban across, for example, parts of Afghanistan and the surrounding countries. With their firebrand version of cultural misogyny and confused, culturally-based reading of Islam, they have come to represent to the Western eye the Islamic bogeymen wanting the whole world to submit to

---

57 See the Wikipedia entry for Salman Rushdie at http://en.wikipedia.org/wiki/Salman_Rushdie. I accessed this on 20 Mar 13.
58 Figures vary depending on source but the US Department of Homeland Security's START program at the University of Maryland quotes 2997 at http://www.start.umd.edu/
59 Jyllands-Posten (30 September 2005) one of the principal daily newspapers in Denmark

their narrow interpretation of *Shari'ah* (if it is even a valid interpretation of Shari'ah) and they are willing to murder people who disagree.

In Belgium 'Shari'ah4Belgium' is active, especially among disillusioned young Muslims using social media (blogs, Tweets and Facebook). These groups (no doubt aided by certain sectors of the Western media) have caused *Shari'ah* to become associated in the Western mind with forced marriages, honour killings, beheadings, forced veiling and even the stoning of women as punishment for having been raped. There is no doubt that these things happen but they are based on interpretations of Shari'ah that suit misogynistic psychopaths with guns and are not followed by the majority of Muslims who condemn them in the strongest terms, even if the condemnations are marginalised by the same thugs who use terror as a way of controlling the conversation.[60]

There Are "Good Muslim" Stories

It should be clear but often isn't that many of the types of behaviour described (ignoring the media hype and the inflated hyperbole of some blog commentators) are not representative of Islam or Muslims in general or *Shari'ah*. For example, in the UK we can find the responses from the Muslim community to such worrying trends as such as Muslim 'street patrols' in Tower Hamlets in London. An imam from Tower Hamlets, Sheikh Shams Ad Duha, is clear in his response that Muslims in non-Muslim states must obey the laws and traditions of the countries in which they live.[61] The need to respond quickly and categorically in the condemnation of atrocities carried out in the name of Islam appears to have been learned. The response to the violent and bloody massacre of the young British soldier, Lee Rigby, outside his barracks in Woolwich, London, was unequivocal. This type of behaviour is not just not acceptable under Islam it is forbidden.

Shari'ah is a Way of Life

As has been described in the short history of Islam in Chapter 3, Shari'ah is 'the Way' through life for Muslims. It is Islamic Law derived from the Holy Quran, the Sunnah of the Prophet and His Companions and scholarship on the part of Islamic jurists. It is a form of law that governs everything that a good Muslim must do and even should do every day, wherever they are. *Shari'ah* governs how Muslims worship and how often they worship, how they manage relationships between people, what they can and cannot do in

---

[60] http://www.bbc.co.uk/news/world-middle-east-23139784 shows an example of this under the headline "Syria crisis : Sharia law spreading in rebel areas". (Retrieved 2 Jul 13)

[61] http://www.youtube.com/watch?v=fpDJTBBwrKM&list=UUktmxFXANF_WIyFdB77eg3w&index=33. This YouTube video is a short, and enlightening, lecture after Friday prayers in Tower Hamlets, London. The Imam is Shaykh Shams Ad Duha. I accessed this on 20 Mar 13. The expected behaviour of a Muslim under Shari'ah is clearly stated from 12 minutes 30 seconds onwards. At the same time, the Shaykh is clear that we need to acknowledge that Islam is 'missionary' in its outlook – in the same way that Christianity is missionary in its outlook. The clear desire is that the whole of the human race comes to see the 'rightness' of the Islamic way. It is, however, forbidden under Shari'ah to force people to adopt a Muslim way of life

many given circumstances. It forbids them to eat certain food and to partake of intoxicants such as alcohol and tobacco and it even requires them to eat and drink differently at certain times of the year, for example, during Ramadan. For the everyday Muslim, *Shari'ah* provides the guiding principles of their lives and how they manage themselves as God's lieutenants on Earth. It is a powerful, socially-cohesive and generally clear narrative that, unlike the abstraction that Western law can appear at times to be, is part of the fabric of everyday life. For Muslims *Shari'ah*'s strength derives from knowing that in following the tenets of the law God will judge you well when you die. *Shari'ah* is not about how the State will treat you while you are alive. However, it must be remembered that a **Muslim state is a theocracy** – the source of all law is the Quran. Any democratic warrant is subordinate to that. This means that the State is a powerful element in a Muslim's life and is responsible for ensuring *Shari'ah* is followed by the Muslims under its aegis.

Ahkam

Everything that a believing Muslim does or will do at some point in his life will fall into one of five categories[62] under Islamic Law[63], with a stepped scale from Obligatory to Forbidden from Wajib to Haram.

English	Arabic	Example
Obligatory	Wajib	Daily prayer (salah), a onetime pilgrimage to Mecca, Hajj
Recommended	Mustahabb	Reading suras of the Koran. Fulfilment rewarded; no
Permissible	Mubah	Shari'ah has nothing to say on the subject
Disliked	Makruh	Using too much water for daily ablutions
Forbidden	Haram	Sinful things, eg murder, pre-marital sex, and charging interest

Money is a Medium of Exchange Only

Within this context, *Shari'ah* is clear on the subject of finance. Firstly, money is a medium of exchange that facilitates trade between people and communities and it is forbidden that money is loaned out with the expectation of receiving interest. In *Shari'ah*, interest is declared as *Riba* (excess) and you are forbidden to charge interest or to engage in any contract where interest may be charged. Secondly, all business between two parties is to be conducted in a fair, open and honest manner with profits and losses shared by both sides. All of this is guided by the principles enshrined in *Shari'ah*.

---

[62] See the YouTube video at http://www.youtube.com/watch?v=wqGVtybEEXk. This is one from a series of lectures given by Sheikh Haceen Chebaani from the Islamic Information Society of Calgary in Canada. I accessed this on 18 Mar 13.

[63] See the Wikipedia entry for Ahkam at http://en.wikipedia.org/wiki/Ahkam

Islamic Finance in the Modern World

Why has Islamic Finance been the subject of such a rise in popularity over recent decades - a popularity that has extended to the creation of a Dow Jones Index for Shari'ah compatible products?

In her book, "La Finance Islamique", Geneviève Causse-Broquet[64], outlines several possible reasons.

Independence of Islamic states post WW2

Following World War 2 (1939-1945), there was a lot of nationalistic pressure to end Western colonialism. This was certainly true in the Muslim-dominated countries, especially as they became aware of the value of the oil buried beneath the sands in their countries and the fact that most of the money generated was been used to enrich people in foreign lands. This was exacerbated by the behaviour of Western countries, including the installation of what were, in effect, puppet governments, while foreign oil companies took the oil and the money derived from it away. This was made easy as the oil was denominated in dollars, a currency controlled by a powerful nation. This led to strong nationalist movements forming in, for example, Iran and Egypt.

11 September 2011- Fears of Financial Sequestration

Following the creation of OPEC and the various oil crises of the 1970s, some clans in the middle-East, notably the family Saud, became immensely rich. The increase in money pouring into family coffers (with the family Saud, the concept of state equates to family) and national treasuries resulted in money being invested in different parts of the world notably in the USA.

When Al-Qaeda attacked the World Trade Centre in 2001, a lot of middle-Eastern money was repatriated as it was feared that reprisal against Muslims would include the sequestration of funds belonging to Muslim states by authorities in the US.

Petrol Money and High Currency Liquidity

The vast liquidity in these states led to the creation of new financial centres in the Middle-East, notably in Saudi Arabia and Bahrain. These funds were managed according to *Shari'ah* principles and consequently had to be invested in the real economy in order to make a profit. The money could not be loaned out at interest. Islamic Finance on a global scale was giving its modern impetus in the Middle East and its centre is recognised to be in Bahrain, which is the headquarters, for example, of the Accounting and Auditing Organisation for Islamic Financial Institutions (AAOIFI).

Push for Equitable Finance without Interest Payments

There is a strong sense of community (ummah) within Islam. As a result, Ahmad Elnaggar created in Mit Ghamr,

---

[64] La Finance Islamique : Causse-Broquet, Geneviève : Revue Banque Edition 2009

> *...the first modern experiment with Islamic banking was undertaken in Egypt ...the pioneering effort, led by Ahmad Elnaggar, took the form of a savings bank based on profit-sharing in the Egyptian town of Mit Ghamr in 1963. This experiment lasted until 1967, by which time there were nine such banks in country. In 1972, the* Mit Ghamr *Savings project became part of Nasr Social Bank which [is]still in business in Egypt.*

Under *Shari'ah*, money is the medium of exchange and must be used to improve life in the community (at whatever scale you define community). The hoarding of money is forbidden and investment must not be in contradiction to *Shari'ah* principles.

It was estimated in 2010 that IF represented about $1000 billion worldwide – that was at the time less than 1% of the global total but the current growth figure is estimated at around 15%.

Features of the Islamic Economic System and Social Principles

What are the values and principles that form the core of Shari'ah-compliant financing? In her book, Causse-Broquet summarizes what she calls Islamic economic and social principles under the following headings:[65]

- Vicegerency – Man is God's lieutenant on Earth and he must look after it. In the end men do not possess property in an absolute (speaking from a Western legal perspective) sense because it all belongs to God.
- Work Ethic – Work is considered as an obligation and a responsibility because:

  And that there is not for man except that [good] for which he strives and that his effort is going to be seen[66]

- Community Spirit and Solidarity – Over the centuries, different factors have produced in the West a strong, almost inalienable, sense of individualism. Whether this is through capitalism, the 'protestant work ethic' or the development of great conurbations or other factors is open for debate. However, in the Muslim world, collectivism is the predominant way of being. This means that there is great peer-pressure placed on any one individual's behaviour. This means that solidarity and social justice are the privileged values within Islam. For example, the paying of tax (Zakat) is a civic and religious duty.

  Indeed, those who believe and do righteous deeds and establish prayer and give zakat[67] will have their reward with their Lord, and there will be no fear concerning them, nor will they grieve.[68]

- Time cannot be the sole basis of any commercial transaction. Without work any remuneration based on Time is illicit.
- Role of Money – Riches and money have always been controversial in the world's religions. A particular feature of Islam is that money is not an object that can be sold or loaned as it has no value in itself. No contract is legitimate if it allows the creation of money without an associated creation of physical capital and productive work. Money is not to be hoarded for its own sake. In the both the Koran and the New Testament this is made clear:

---

[65] Causse-Broquet op cit p 31

[66] Sura 53 (39-40)

[67] **Zakat** "that which purifies"), is the giving of a fixed portion of one's wealth as a tax, generally to the administration or government and is one of the Five Pillars of Islam http://en.wikipedia.org/wiki/Zak%C4%81t accessed 14 Mar 2013

[68] Sura 2 (277)

> **Woe to every scorner and mocker who collects wealth and [continuously] counts it. He thinks that his wealth will make him immortal. No! He will surely be thrown into the Crusher**[69]
>
> **You cannot serve God and money**[70]

These principles derive from the primary objectives (Maqasid) of Shari'ah (that is, what is it that Shari'ah is aiming to protect and preserve). Ayub lists these primary objectives as follows[71]:

- Religion
- Life
- Progeny (the family unit)
- Property [including property]
- Intellect
- Honour

With respect to religion, "Shari'ah makes it the responsibility of the [Muslim] State to implement Shari'ah requirements in respect of beliefs"[72]. From a Western perspective, with our cherished separation of Church and State, it is important to remember that, in a Muslim State, there is no concept of the separation of state and religion.

Ayub continues:

"The protection and preservation of human life refers to the sanctity of life as emphasized in the Qur'an and Sunnah. There is the law of Qisas to punish those who cause any harm to human life. This objective also refers to the provision of basic necessities to all human beings.

The protection of progeny or the family unit relates to marriage and the family institution, whose purposes are: procreation, protection against lack of chastity and the proper upbringing of children, enabling them to become good human beings and Muslims and to bring peace and tranquillity to society. [This can be achieved by] the promotion of the marriage contract, tenets relating to family life and the prohibition of adultery.

The protection of wealth and property refers to the sanctity of the wealth of all members of society, with an emphasis on valid (Halal) earning and discouragement of a concentration of wealth leading to a vast gap between the poor and the rich and the inability of the former to meet their basic needs of food, health and fundamental education. For this purpose, Islam provides a comprehensive law governing Mu'amalat or transactions among members of a society."

Ayub then argues that these primary requirements (although he does not discuss intellect and honour further) lead to secondary objectives. These are:

- The establishment of justice and equity in society.

---

[69] Sura 104 (1-4)

[70] Gospel According to Matthew : Chapter 6 Verse 24

[71] Ayub *op cit* p 23

[72] *op cit* p 23

- The promotion of social security, mutual help and solidarity, particularly to help the poor and the needy in meeting their basic needs.
- The maintenance of peace and security.
- The promotion of cooperation in matters of goodness and prohibition of evil deeds and actions.
- The promotion of supreme universal moral values and all actions necessary for the preservation and authority of nature.

Although it would be hard to argue against the first 3 points above, the two remaining points leave the path open to discussions on the nature of good and evil and the exact nature of "supreme universal moral values". This is not the place for that discussion and the next section looks at how an Islamic economic system can be derived from Shari'ah principles.

Islamic Economics

Islam requires rulers and various regulators in an economic system, "protect the masses from harm and hardships caused by unscrupulous factors in society through strong and effective laws... The State **must** [my emphasis] curb also institutional and other malpractices"[73] As a system based on a revealed text and its associated commentaries, Islamic economics is necessarily a system that is driven by different imperatives to the Western model. These imperatives are, according to M A Mannan,[74] "ideological, economic, social, ethical, political, historical and international" and in his view "...Islamic economics cannot remain neutral between different ends. It is concerned with what is and what *ought* to be, in the light of the Shari'ah".

It must also be remembered that Islamic economics is not a new idea. It derives from a period when the nominally Christian West was passing through a dark era after the decline of Rome and the subsequent invasions by various barbarian hordes. During this "Golden Age of Islam":

> *Great ports provided the Muslim World with ships, dockyards, and seafaring populations. There were three enormous complexes: first, shipping in the Persian Gulf and the Red Sea, which Arab and Persian sailors opened up towards the Indian Ocean and which was complemented by the river-boats of the Euphrates and Tigris; next, the ports of Syria and Egypt, foremost of which was Alexandria, backed by the river-boats of the Nile; finally, the ports on the Sicilian Strait and the Strait of Gibraltar, supported by the river-boats on the Guadalquivir[75]
> . Caravan towns also possessed transport systems which dominated the Mesopotamian routes (running westwards*

---

73 Ayub op cit p 25

74 Mannan, M.A. (1984) The Making of Islamic Economic Society. International Association for Islamic Banks, Cairo, pp 5–74

75 The Guadalquivir is a Spanish river that flows into the Atlantic Ocean to the west of the Strait of Gibraltar. Its name derives from the Arabic Wadi-al-Kabir, which means the great valley. It is about 657 km long and is one of the longest rivers in Spain.

towards Syria and eastwards towards Iran and central Asia), the Arabian routes, and the Berber trading routes crossing the Sahara.[76]

This golden era lasted until the Muslim World received:

> *"...a mortal blow in the form of the crises, the disturbances, the invasions of the second half of the eleventh century. [These crises] impeded the powerful flow of trade, thereby provoking the decline of the cities. Henceforward the Muslim World was not a united whole, but divided. There was a Turkish Islam, a Persian Islam, a Syrian Islam, an Egyptian Islam, and a Maghreb Islam. Gone was the single Muslim civilization and in its place was a resurgence of regional particularisms, embodied in a number of different Muslim civilizations"*[77]

In Europe, the Holy Roman Empire backed by the Roman Catholic Church, (finding along the way the Kingdom of France to be an Earthly irritation) was the overarching, if not completely dominant, religious and political force up until the Enlightenment period. During the nineteenth century there was a re-emergence of Islamic Finance "...as an intelligent academic pursuit... [that led to a process]... of defining modern economic thought in the light of the principles of Islam"[78]. That this revival and re-evaluation of Islamic economics coincided with a period denoted in English, if not European history, as the Industrial Revolution and the later formulation of Engels and Marx's "The Communist Manifesto" (1848) and later of Marx's Capital (1867) is, on reflection, not in the least surprising.

Islamic economics is an example of welfare (or normative) economics in which policy recommendations must involve some value judgements.

> *"The Islamic approach is that economic development and creation of abundant wealth are means to satisfy human needs and support society. These are not sought for boasting or spending in offence, arrogance or oppression. Linking this world with the Hereafter, Islam enjoins Muslims to seek the Hereafter through what they earn and not to forget their share of the worldly life."* The Holy Qur'an says:

> **"And seek the abode of the Hereafter in that which Allah has given you, and do not neglect your portion of worldly life, and be kind as Allah has been kind to you, and seek not disorder/corruption in the earth". (28: 77)**

> *Therefore, Islamic rules of economics make it binding for human beings not only to abide by the Shari'ah tenets relating to dos and don'ts but also to keep in mind the impact of their activities on others and society as a whole.*[79]

---

76 Lombard, Maurice, The Golden Age of Islam (1971) p9

[77] *ibid* pp 10-11

[78] Ayub *op cit* p 29

Ayub makes the point that the currently worked-out version of the Islamic economic system is different from both the capitalistic and socialistic systems[80] calling it an integrated model which provides, "a positive motivation for economic activities, steered by the concept of a fair balance between material and spiritual needs and between the individual's and society's needs.[81]

Objective of the Islamic Economic System

Ayub is clear that Islamic economics "takes its roots from the belief that all resources in the world belong to its Creator, One God; human beings are holding these resources in trust…Behaving as vicegerent of the Creator.[82] He is also clear about what Islamic economics is trying to achieve:

> *The objective of the Islamic economic system, like any other economic system, is the realization of efficiency and equity in allocation and distribution of resources, for which it recognizes the role of market forces and the freedom of individuals. But it also recognizes the possible adverse impact of the totally unregulated market on various sections of society, particularly the poor and the disadvantaged. The pure materialistic "positive" approach has never been capable of serving social interests and realizing such goals. The "invisible hand" of market forces, as contended by Adam Smith, has failed to fulfil the social obligations required for the ultimate socio-economic outcome of human actions. Hence, Islamic economics provides ample room for State intervention to achieve an optimal mix of functioning of market players guided by individual self-interest and serving the social interest by the State's facilitation and overseeing activities.*
>
> *The urge for maximization of wealth by individuals without taking care of its impact on the well-being of others or society as a whole cannot generate long-term sustainable growth and well-being of individuals or societies. Therefore, both positive and normative objectives are to be realized through market functioning supported by State facilitation and intervention aimed at realization of socio-economic goals like need-fulfilment, an optimum and stable growth rate, equitable distribution of income and wealth with class and ecological coherence.[83]*

Within this context, "Man has to enjoy and use wealth under Allah's command. Islam has given the individual the freedom to earn a livelihood." In the same way, every individual has "the right to enjoy whatever wealth he

---

[79] *ibid* p 30
[80] Islamic Economics does contain elements of both, as will become clear.
[81] Ayub *op cit* p32
[82] op cit p 33
[83] *ibid* p 32

has earned by legal means and whatever wealth he has received through the Islamic law of inheritance." To allow individuals to acquire property and wealth, Islamic law facilitates the" legal means of ownership and its transfer through a variety of contracts."[84] General rules for these contracts have also "been defined in detail with the possibility of resolving any contemporary issues through Ijtihad, subject to observance of allowed limits. These rules allow man to utilize the resources by consuming them, benefiting from them or exchanging them via a number of contracts like sale, loan, lease or gift." Along with property rights, income and profit entitlement are [also] established in Islamic economics. This must occur through… effort, work or taking responsibility (Dhaman) and distribution [through] partnership, trade, joint ventures and loans…" and by "various vehicles of transfer incomes like grants and Zakat, and the control of waste. Hence, the Islamic economy has a linkage between the market functions of productive involvement and growth and the institutional functions of policy and control."[85]

In summary then, there is in the Islamic economic system:

- Ownership of commodities and wealth
- Transfer of ownership
- Distribution of wealth among the people

According to Ayub, within the Islamic framework, the Holy Qur'an and Sunnah lead to economic principles that, "encourage human beings' development, enforce justice, stop exploitation **and tend to set up a contented and satisfied society**[86] [my emphasis] that can be termed a real welfare society[87].[88] In addition to achieving optimum produce in both public and private sectors, allocation and distribution of resources and produce must take a course that fulfils the basic human needs of all, irrespective of the colour, race and/or creed of the people. The fulfilment of basic needs makes society tranquil, comfortable, healthy and efficient, and able to contribute properly towards the realization and perpetuation of human welfare."[89]

---

[84] *ibid* p 33

[85] *ibid* p 34

[86] It goes without saying that this is one particular view of what makes a contented and satisfied society and it is a view derived from a belief in an all-powerful creator. Disappointingly, however, Ayub then goes on, creating a wonderful straw man argument in the process, to make the declaration that it is a "secular core value" to oppose this Islamic view of "moderation"! Secularism is separation of church and state. There is no principle in secularism that denies the necessities of life to anyone. Nor is there any declaration that opposes the minimization of the hardships of life. Islamic economics contains some excellent ideas well worth studying in the current financial crisis, however, promoting these ideas by creating false and irrelevant arguments against secularism do nothing but diminish Dr Ayub's standing as an intellectual.

[87] Ayub does not provide empirical evidence for this view. He even quotes an Islamic economist, Umer Chapra, who points out in his article that « There is, however, no theoretical macroeconomic model that would show how Islamic values and institutions, and different sectors of the economy, society and polity would interact to realize this vision…it has not been possible to establish the relationship among the macroeconomic goals and the behaviour of different economic agents and the kind of socio-economic and political reform that the realization of goals may require »

[88] Chapra, M. Umer (2000) "Is it Necessary to Have Islamic Economics?" The Journal of Socioeconomics, 29, pp 21–37

Within the Islamic worldview, "If some individuals are unable to earn and fulfil their needs, Shari´ah obliges their fellow beings – depending upon the nature of the relationship like neighbours, relatives, etc. – to support them in fulfilling their basic needs. If there is nobody to support such people, Islam obliges the State to be responsible for the support of all citizens, particularly mentally or physically disabled people and the destitute."

---

[89] *ibid* p 34

Islamic Finance – Principles and Ethics

Islamic financial activity is growing in two ways; through the creation of new products and the return of old ones. In all cases, the constraint is *Shari'ah* which makes it necessary, when creating new financial products, to avoid any prohibitions arising from Islamic economic and social principles. That is:

> *"all business and financial contracts in the framework of Islamic finance have to conform to the Shari'ah rules with the objective of helping to achieve Maqasid [90] al Shari'ah"[91]*

Islamic Versus "Western" Capitalism

Islamic Economics and its associated financial systems are, like the western system, capital-based. The MAJOR difference[92] between the two systems derives from the Quranic injunction against Riba (an excess paid for borrowing something - not necessarily money - over time) and which, in the western system, corresponds to interest paid for money borrowed or interest paid for money lent. This injunction on the charging of interest has, as a consequence, in the distribution of income and wealth that:

> *"...none of the factors of production is deprived of its share nor does it exploit any other. Land, labour and capital jointly create value. As a result, the land-owner, the labourer and the owner of capital should jointly share the produce. The distinctive feature of the Islamic system is that capital has to bear the loss, if any. In addition to this, Islam compulsorily retains a portion of the produced wealth as Zakat for those who are prevented from contributing their share in production due to any social, physical or economic handicap."[93]*

Criticism

Of course, there is, in the quote from Ayub, an assumption that does not hold up to even a brief examination. In claiming that the **distinctive** feature of the Islamic system is that "capital has to take the loss" he completely ignores the fact that there are within the Western system a significant number of capitalists (entrepreneurs) who put their capital at risk in giving support to start-ups and other expanding, or even struggling businesses for a share in the profits of the company[94]. This support may be financial or take the form of advice on how best to run a company to ensure that it is successful. If the business fails, they accept the loss. They then learn the lessons and move on to the next project. This behaviour is entirely voluntary, there is no State requiring that they do this – although support may be available if they do. To

---

[90] Maq¯asid refers to the objectives of Shari'ah

[91] Ayub op cit page 21

[92] There are several others that will be discussed in detail later

[93] *ibid* p 35

[94] For example, the popularity of the BBC's « Dragon's Den » is a witness to this form of capitalism

suggest that this type of behaviour is distinctively Islamic is to view the world with through ideological blinkers.

The reason for his unsupportable claim (that it is only under Islamic Finance that capital has to take the loss) becomes clear in his description of "the concept of capital". He claims that "...a different treatment of capital in the conventional economic theory...narrows down the concept by restricting capital to borrowed money". According to Ayub then, all capital in the western system is money borrowed at interest. This is something that is demonstrably not true.

> *This concept of capital as only money loaned out at interest by banks or other organisations seeking a profit without doing any real work by charging interest based only on money and time, "which is discarded by Islam" is another straw man argument designed to persuade the unwary or to preach to the converted.*

That a large amount of capital is available in this fashion is beyond doubt, but to claim that only Islamic Finance has a system where capital takes the loss is at best naïve and undeserving of Ayub's intellect and at worst dishonest. We do recognise in the "West" human capital and intellect and the intangible assets held by companies in the form of experience among employees and such legal constructs as patents and copyright.

The point, I believe, that Ayub wanted to make is that under the Islamic system money is not treated as capital as it is useful only when it is brought together with land and labour. Money on its own is without value and cannot claim "rent" for its use. On the other hand, land and labour are still useful and able to do real work in the absence of money.

As we will see later, Islamic Finance has a number of business arrangements and contract types that have been created to meet Shari'ah requirements and most notably the absolute injunction on the charging or paying of interest. Just as important is the idea that only by working hard and accepting a risk can an honest profit be made in a business operating under the Islamic economic system. Once again, Ayub gives an excellent summary:

> *"Profit, according to Islamic theory, is the result of the productivity of capital that an entrepreneur has invested or a reward for his workmanship or for shouldering responsibility. As capital provider he has to bear the loss, if any, and as entrepreneur he has to pay the wages, rentals and other expenses and gets the residual, if any. All participants in a joint business have similar rights and liabilities according to the nature of the activity or the terms of the agreement."[95]*

All Shari'ah-Compliant Products are allowed

There are 5 general prohibitions:
- Prohibition on the charging of interest – (*riba*)

---

[95] *ibid* p 42

- Prohibition on contracts involving incertitude, cheating and risk – (*gharar*)
- Enrichment for its own sake
- Speculation – (*maysir*)
- Illicit Activities

Prohibition of Riba

As discussed earlier when outlining the position of the monotheistic religions on the issue of usury, Riba is clearly prohibited in the Qur'an and Sunnah. All Muslim sects consider indulgence in riba-based transactions to be a severe sin. To understand riba and provide a clearer view of riba as an excess of something granted over time, Muslim scholars often refer to traditions (Hadith). One of the clearest is:

> *"The holy Prophet said, 'Gold for gold, silver for silver, wheat for wheat, barley for barley, dates for dates and salt for salt – like for like, equal for equal, and hand to hand; if the commodities differ, then you may sell as you wish, provided that the exchange is hand to hand.'"*

So the prohibition occurs only if one receives an excess of the same thing. If the items to be exchanged are different then it is an exchange of goods. If you wish to exchange, for example dates for dates, you must exchange the same weight in dates, even if the quality is different. If you want to distinguish between different quality dates, you must first exchange one set of dates for dirhams (money) and then use the dirhams to buy dates of the other quality. The two separate transactions, dates for dirhams and then dirhams for dates, do not create riba when taken together, even if the weight of dates exchanged is different.

The prohibition on *Riba* is perhaps the best known aspect of Islamic Finance among those who have encountered it. Certainly, a lot of work has been done by Islamic scholars to ensure that any transaction can be shown to be free of the taint of riba making it appear as the *sine qua non* of the Islamic financial system. The prohibition on *riba* is an essential characteristic of Islamic Finance although it is not unique to Islam as a religion as will be discussed later.

The form of *riba* that we understand as interest in the Western formulation is:

> ...*all interest stipulated **contractually** and calculated **beforehand** on the basis of the **initial capital** borrowed and the **period** of the loan agreed **without any connection to the final outcome** of the operation being financed.*[96]

That is, money itself, without any effort made on the part of the lenders, is able to generate more money. It is a guaranteed profit. It is this guarantee of profit for no risk taken (assuming that the lender pays the capital and interest as required in the contract) that is unacceptable before Allah.

---

[96] Causse-Broquet op cit p34 (my translation from French)

Due to the role assigned to money in Islam, money in itself is non-productive. It cannot generate revenue over time. Although there are divergences of thought within Islam, the majority legal opinion from the High Commission for the Interpretation of the Koran in Saudi Arabia is that all transactions involving interest are forbidden as is clearly written in the Koran (Sura 2:275).

As mentioned in the introduction, "indulging in Riba-based transactions is tantamount to being at war with Allah (SWT) and His Messenger, which no one should even think of."[97] The principle given in the Quran (Suras 2:278 and 279) is that,

> "...for both loans and debts, the creditor has the right to the Ra'asul-m⁻al (principal amount) only; in the former case, exactly the amount given as the loan and in the latter case, the liability or the amount of debt generated from the credit transaction. Any amount, big or small, over and above the principal of loan or debt would be Riba"[98]

The difference between profit and interest

Within the *Shari'ah* context, all income and earnings, salaries and wages, remuneration and profits, usury[99] and interest, rent and hire and so on can be categorized either as:

- Profit from trade and business along with its liability – which is permitted (halal)
- Return on cash or a converted form of cash[100] without bearing liability in terms of the result of deployed cash or capital – which is prohibited (haram)

The belief, within the Islamic Finance system, is that if a loan is given on the basis of interest:

- The risk is not shared equally since only the borrower bears the risk. It is from here that social injustice arises.
- The term of the loan is fixed, so you are paying for time – which is God's creation and property – not Man's
- The return is based solely on the amount of money borrowed; the money makes money; this is against nature[101].

Trade without Interest

Interest appears almost everywhere in the Western system but "God has permitted trade and prohibited Riba"[102]. After a price has been stipulated it

---

[97] Ayub *op cit* p 47

[98] *ibid*

[99] Usury used to mean any interest, it has now taken the meaning of excessive interest (if that has any meaning)

[100] For example, something that has been bought using cash

[101] Money is considered, as it is in some verses of the Bible as barren – it cannot bear fruit in and of itself

[102] Holy Qur'an (Sura 2 :275)

cannot change. This means, for those interested in following the Quran's injunction on Riba, that there needs to be a clear manner in which any business transaction can be shown to be legitimate under Shari'ah (that is, halal). What are the features that distinguish interest-bearing transactions from those that do not? Any business contract can be placed into one of three categories:

- Sales or Purchase that is cash or credit
- Loaning
- Leasing

When any of these types of contract are executed (the contracts, of course, do not have to be written ones) there are different implications with respect to the transfer of ownership, risk and liability.

Sale

In a sale (Bai' in Islamic Finance) ownership of the item that is sold is transferred to the buyer **at the time that the sale is executed**. This transfer is definite and permanent and it does not matter if the price is paid **on the spot** or if the payment is **deferred**. The price paid will, if any kind of useful economy is to develop, include an appropriate profit margin for the seller. It is a fundamental tenet of Islamic Finance that the price cannot change after the contract has been executed even if the payment has been deferred and the buyer has not made the payment on time. Any additional charge is riba (extra money taken on the basis of the passage of time). Anyone who sells on credit will, therefore, need an appropriate risk management strategy.

Loan

A loan (Hiba) leads to the temporary transfer of ownership of goods/assets free of any charge. The debtor is liable to return the borrowed item or pay back the same asset to the lender. All loans are always free of any charge.

Lease

Leasing (Ijarah) is a transaction in which the ownership of the leased asset does not transfer when the contract is executed. Only the freedom to use the item leased is transferred – this use being referred to as the usufruct. The usufruct is made available to the lessee in return for the payment of rent. The owner of the leased asset is liable for the expenses relating to ownership and also the loss of the asset. Leasing is only used when the asset that is leased will not change its form or be used up in the process of putting them to use. For example, you cannot lease yarn to make clothes because the weaver cannot return the yarn at the end of the leasing contract. Its form will have been changed. Yarn would have to be bought or sold.

Profit and Loss Sharing - Not Interest

The prohibition of interest and the sharing of profit and loss go well together. There are good arguments that charging interest (however low it value will tend to widen the gap between the rich and the poor. The famous translator of the Qur'an into English, Allama Yusuf Ali, uses clear language to indicate the disdain with which those who lend money at interest are held:

> *"Whereas legitimate trade or industry increases the prosperity and stability of men and nations, dependence over usury would merely encourage a race of idlers, cruel bloodsuckers and worthless fellows who do not know their own good and therefore are akin to madmen"*[103]

Ayub follows this up by highlighting the fact that any rate above zero is usury. "The distinction between interest and usury is made just to deceive mankind and to allow the same old robbery in a more presentable form"[104]

To avoid any accusations of charging Riba bank with capital to lend in the form of money need to lend it in a manner that is fully-conformant to Islamic Finance principles. As the bank has to make some profit 5it has to pay its own rent, salaries and other costs after all), the bank and the lender, enter into an agreement to become partners. Each will agree to a fixed portion of the profits from the work of the lender (entrepreneur). In this way it should be clear that **it is the method** in which the added-value for the bank has been generated that makes the difference. With an interest-based system, the bank will always get its money and some 'profit' back, regardless of how well or badly the lender manages the project for which the money has been loaned (assuming that the lender continues to pay). In a profit and loss sharing system, the bank runs the risk of losing money (or at least not making a profit) if the project does not go well. The bank puts a lot of trust in the lender to make good use of the money for the project for which the money has been loaned. Likewise, if the lender wants to lend again he will have to show that he is worthy of the trust placed in him by the lender. This type of contract is discussed in more detail later. For now, the point about not charging interest on money capital has, I think, been clearly made and:

> *"Hence, there is no place for "interest". That is to say, a person who wants to invest his money in any business must take the risk of loss, only then is he entitled to profit. The one who provides land gets rent or revenue, and the provider of labour gets a salary or wages. Should any joint business fail, the provider of capital would lose his money, the provider of land would lose rent and the provider of labour would lose salary. If a man owns his business, he gets or loses all three rewards."*[105]

---

[103] Without doubt the rhetoric is powerful and the language potentially accurate but what of a capitalist who is also engaged in legitimate trade? That this is true seems to be borne out by the increasing debt burden of the Third World countries crippled by debt interest payments passing out the value of their countries to meet financial obligations that never seem to go away

[104] Ayub *op cit* p55

[105] Ibid p 57

Prohibition of Gharar

Gharar refers to the uncertainty or hazard caused by lack of clarity regarding the subject or price of a contract or exchange and may be present in the following examples:

- A party signing a contact without been clear about its significance
- A payment to be made by one of the contracting parties under some conditions
- The cost of the contract being unclear at the time of signature

Any sale or business contract that entails an element of gharar is prohibited. Whereas uncertainty cannot be completely avoided in business (an element of risk is required for a legitimate profit) too much will render a transaction Haram. Unfortunately, there is not a clear definition of what is an acceptable level of gharar. Most advice proceeds by the use of examples. These examples can then be used to help decision-making in novel situations.

Examples

Several religious opinions (*hadiths*) give examples:

- The sale of a camel that is not yet born
- The sale of wool that is still on an animal
- The sale of a bird that is still on the wing

Modern day examples may include:

- Purchase/sale of some object/material where the price will be fixed later
- Purchase/sale of a house where the characteristics will be decided later

No Sale

Although it is an ongoing area of research with Islamic Finance, in order to avoid uncertainty, Islamic law denies a merchant the power to sell in the following three situations:

- Things which, as the object of a legal transaction, do not exist
- Things which exist but which are not in possession of the seller or the availability of which may not be expected
- Things which are exchanged on the basis of uncertain delivery and payment

Gharar through Ignorance or Deception

The following types of contract would also be illegal due to the presence of gharar:

- Selling goods that the seller is unable to deliver
- Making contract conditional on an unknown event

- Making contracts too complex to clearly define rights and responsibilities
- Selling goods based on false description

Car Servicing

A good example comes from Sheikh Haceen Chebaani[106]. He describes the common problem encountered when a car is taken in to be serviced. We never know what work needs to be carried out nor exactly the price in advance. As a price cannot be quoted, the contract is technically *gharar* and we may be unpleasantly surprised by the final bill. However, there is often no choice. The garage owner may not be able to say what the exact cost will be because the exact nature of the problem has not been discovered. It is possible that this tricky issue could be solved by giving a possible range for the price.

It is, however, permitted to buy/sell standard goods that are delivered regularly at the end of a given period where the actual price depends on an unspecified market price. In the real economy, the avoidance of *gharar* is clearly difficult, especially in big projects spanning several months or even years. What is needed is that the utmost effort be made to comply with the spirit of *Shari'ah*. Unlike Riba where the slightest involvement of Riba renders a transaction non-Shari'ah compliant, some degree of uncertainty is acceptable with the Islamic Finance context.

Prohibition of *Maisir/Qimar* (Games of Chance)

Easily available wealth or the acquisition of wealth by chance or with ease, even if it doesn't deprive the other side is prohibited. The two words are usually interchangeable in Arabic but Islamic jurists make Qimar a subset of Maisir. Maisir means wishing something valuable with ease and without paying an equivalent compensation for it or without working for it. The Quran is clear:

> O you who believe! Intoxicants and gambling, sacrificing to stones and divination by arrows, are abominable actions of Satan; so abstain from them, that you may prosper."(5: 90)

> "Satan intends to excite enmity and hatred among you with intoxicants and gambling, and hinder you from the remembrance of Allah, and from prayer; will ye not then abstain? (5: 91)

It is clear, then, that lotteries operated by governments, financial institutions and NGOs "are repugnant to the tenets of Shari'ah"[107] because the incentives provided to the investors are not the profits accruing on the investment but disproportionate prizes distributed by drawing lots. In this sense the UK National Savings' Premium Bond Scheme is doubly prohibited. The prize

---

[106] See the YouTube video at http://www.youtube.com/watch?v=wqGVtybEEXk. This is one from a series of lectures given by Sheikh Haceen Chebaani from the Islamic Information Society of Calgary in Canada. The time frame is about 4 min 32s to 6 min 54s. I accessed this 18 Mar 13.

[107] Ayub *op cit* p63

money pot is derived from interest on the bonds purchased and the allocation of prizes is as close as possible to random as an electronic engineer can make it.

Prohibition of Illicit Activities

There are activities that are not allowed in Islamic Finance. These products are deemed *haram* as opposed to *halal,* which refers to products and activities that are permitted. The *haram* activities include trade in alcohol, pork meat, armaments and trade with companies that screen the entrepreneur from these and other *haram* activities. This includes using banks that trade with companies that engage in *haram* activities. It is also not permitted to trading speculatively in gold, silver or money.

Business Ethics and Norms under Shari'ah

Shari'ah isn't all about prohibition. For the conduct of economic affairs it has created a set of principles that provide a framework that relates to financial and commercial transactions. The Quran and Sunnah enunciate principles of "...justice, mutual help, free consent and honesty..." between contracting parties such that they avoid, "...fraud, misrepresentation and misstatement of facts and negation of justice or exploitation". If a contract has taken all these factors into account it can be declared valid.

Justice and Fair Dealing

The idea of justice is, like in all revealed religion and secular thought, an important one. The relevant verse from the Qur'an says:

> **"...And let not the enmity and hatred of others make you avoid justice. Be just; that is nearest to piety... (5: 8). Stressing this point, the Qur'an further says: "You who believe stand steadfast before Allah as witness for (truth and) fair play" (4: 135)**

Within Islam, whoever believes in God has to be just with everyone, even enemies. Personal gain at the expense of others is not just and contradicts the following verse in the Qur'an:

> **"And eat up not one another's property unjustly (in any illegal way, e.g. stealing, robbing, deceiving, etc.) nor give bribery to the rulers that you may knowingly eat up a part of the property of others sinfully" (2: 188)**

According to Ayub:

> *Honesty, truthfulness and care for others are the basic lessons taught to Muslims by the Shari'ah, with relatively more emphasis in respect of business transactions. The holy Prophet (pbuh) has said: "The truthful and honest merchant shall be with the Prophets, the truthful and the martyrs on the day of Resurrection." He also said: "It is not lawful for a Muslim to sell to his brother[108] something defective without pointing out the defect"*

All Muslims are required to avoid deception, which, if revealed, would allow any contract to be rescinded,

"Fill the measure when you measure, and weigh with a perfectly good balance" (17:35)

In the interests of justice, lending is a virtuous act under Islam. However, creditors need to be gentle and even give more time to repay a debt if the debtor is genuinely in trouble. This is supported by the words of the Prophet:

"Whoever takes money with the intention of repaying it, Allah would (arrange to) repay it on his behalf, and whoever takes it in order to spoil it, then Allah would spoil him"

There is a difference, however, between an individual behaving like this towards another individual and an institution, such as a bank, which has taken people's money on trust. A bank cannot allow those who wilfully default on their debts to be forgiven in the same way as that would contribute to social problems arising from moral hazard. For this reason, Shari'ah boards that run Islamic banks may, "impose fines on defaulters with the objective of disciplining their clients and as a deterrent against wilful default." The Prophet has said:

"Procrastination (delay) in repaying debts by a wealthy person is injustice"[109]

However, any fine, which might be viewed as Riba (an excess of the money loaned out), must be used for charitable purposes only and cannot be added to the bank's profit and loss account.

Prohibition of Najash (Bidding up Prices)

Justice means that the practice of bidding up the prices at an auction (Najash), without the intention to purchase and take delivery of the commodity, is not permissible. In the view of the prophet, "A Najish (an agent who bids up prices) is a cursed taker of Riba" and "If anyone interferes in the market to create a rise in prices, God has right to cast him face down in Hell". Clearly, these distortions in the market are harmful and must be punished.

Prohibition of Khalabah (Misleading Marketing)

This includes pursuing unaware and simple clients by overstating the quality of a commodity. It is not permissible to present a product as something it is not or too use techniques that may increase sales in the short term but which, in the longer term may bring about "destruction"[110]

---

[108] Brother in this sense means any other Muslim – not a blood relation necessarily
[109] This is attributed by Ayub to Abu Haraira
[110] The word "destruction" is from the Prophet as described by Imam Muslim in his Sahih

Disclosure, Transparency and Facilitating Inspection

One of the most important aspects of doing business is the availability of information. In the Western mathematical models of economics, each actor is assumed to have perfect information. Without this information, the equations and their interpretation have less value. The same is true of Islamic Shari'ah which derives its view from Sura 2:188 (see previous section). Islam considers that the provision of inaccurate or deceptive information is a sin and any contract that has depended on it can be rescinded. Ayub illustrates this:

> *"The holy Prophet (pbuh) once passed by a man who was selling grain [and] He asked him: "How are you selling it?" The man then informed him. The Prophet (pbuh) then put his hand in the heap of grain and found it [was] wet inside. Then he said: "He who deceives other people is not one of us."[111]*

Therefore, to meet the requirements of Shari'ah:

> *"All parties in the market must have enough information about the quality, value of the product, purchasing power of the clients and demand for the product. The wares being sold should be capable of inspection to enable both parties to reasonably know the benefits in case the contract is finalized. For the purpose of transparency, therefore, transactions should be executed within the market or the place where people are aware of the demand and supply situation and are in a position to trade taking into account all relevant information."[112]*

Overall, this is no different to the requirements of the Western economic system. However, with or without the fear of punishment in the Afterlife, it is necessary to implement practical legal oversight to ensure the maximum availability of information to those who need it.

Fulfilling Covenants and Paying Liabilities

Like all contracts those under Islamic law result in rights and liabilities. Each signatory must fulfil the liability created in the contract. Under Shari'ah one is obliged to fulfil not only contracts but also promises and unilateral agreements. Under Shari'ah those that do not fulfil their promises are simply "hypocrites".[113] Contemporary Islamic scholars unanimously consider promises to be binding and promises play an important role in certain Islamic Finance products, for example, Murabahah to Purchase Orderer, Leasing and Diminishing Musharakah. Contracts in general and these particular examples, along with others, will be discussed in more detail in the chapters that follow.

---

[111] Ayub *op cit* p 67
[112] *idem*
[113] This is a paraphrase of Ayub from *op cit* p 67

Mutual Cooperation and Removal of Hardship

Although insurance is an important element of the "Western" model, the idea of mutual aid and indemnification against loss is a holy duty under Shari'ah:

> *Mutual help, solidarity and joint indemnification of losses and harm are other important norms of the Islamic economic framework...Islam cherishes that a person helps others in times of need and prohibits any such action that may cause any loss or harm to others. The Holy Qur'an says:*
>
> **"Assist one another in the doing of good and righteousness. Assist not one another in sin and transgression, and keep your duty to Allah" (5:2)**
>
> *The holy Prophet has encouraged mutual assistance by saying: "The Believers, in their affection, mercy and sympathy towards each other are like one human body – if one of its organs suffers and complains, the entire body responds with insomnia and fever"*

A number of practices for the relief of mutual hardship, dating from pre-Islamic times are incorporated into Shari'ah. These practices have their roots in familial and tribal schemes for mutual help. The Islamic version of insurance, referred to as Takaful derives from "Dhaman Khatr al-Tariq" whereby:

> *Losses suffered by traders during journeys due to hazards on trade routes were indemnified from jointly created funds. Islam accepted this principle of reciprocal compensation and joint responsibility.[114]*

Free Market and Fair Pricing

Business under Islam is basically a free market model and people are free to enter into any type of halal business or transaction. As implied by the term halal, the does not allow unrestrained freedom to engage in all types of contract. Exchange can only be in permissible commodities and the trade must be carried out in accordance with Shari'ah principles. Later chapter will deal with the details of these rules.

The free market envisaged under Islam is not too different from the Western model.

> *Islam envisages a free market where fair prices are determined by the forces of demand and supply. Prices will be considered fair only if they are the outcome of genuinely free functioning of market forces. There should be no interference in the free play of the forces of demand and supply, so as to avoid injustice on behalf of suppliers of goods and consumers. The holy Prophet has prohibited Ghaban-e-Fahish, which means*

---

[114] idem

selling something at a higher price and giving the impression to the client that he is being charged according to the market rate...

...If a person starts selling his goods in the market at less than the cost price out of his piety and philanthropy, he will be creating problems for others, as a result of which the supply of that commodity may suffer in the future and ultimately people may suffer.[115]

Vested interests (such as cartels) attempting to corner markets will be subject to State intervention to avoid, for example, any attempt to create artificial scarcity for essential commodities, with a view to profiteering.

Islamic Banks and Trade

These prohibitions apply to individuals as well as Islamic banks. Islamic banks have to engage in trade as they cannot lend money at interest. However, while engaged in that trade, they will have to follow the rules laid down in 1988 by the Council of the Islamic Fiqh Academy (based in Jeddah):

• The basic principle in the Quran and the Sunnah of the holy Prophet (pbuh) is that a person should be free to buy and sell and dispose of his possessions and money, within the framework of the Islamic Shari'ah in accordance with the divine Command: ("O you who believe! Consume not each other's property in vanities, unless there is trade based on mutual acceptance").

• There is no restriction on the percentage of profit which a trader may make in his transactions. It is generally left to the merchants themselves, the business environment and the nature of the merchant and of the goods. Care should be given, however, to ethics recommended by Shari'ah, such as moderation, contentment and leniency.

• Shari'ah texts have spelt out the necessity to keep the transactions away from illicit acts like fraud, cheating, deceit, forgery, concealment of actual features and benefits which are detrimental to the well-being of society and individuals.

• Government should not be involved in fixing prices except only when obvious pitfalls are noticed within the market and prices due to artificial factors. In this case, the government should intervene by applying adequate means to get rid of these factors, the causes of defects, excessive price increases and fraud.

Freedom from Dharar (Detriment)

When entering into a contract both sides must provide all the information required to ensure that a contract is fair. Any contract can be rescinded if it

---

[115] Ayub *op cit* p 68

can be shown to lack information where the intention of that lack was to gain a market advantage.

Counter party rights in a contract:

> ...*are much more strongly enforced in the Islamic framework, with a provision of right/option for the informationally-disadvantaged party to reverse its position.* **The State and regulators are duty bound** *to ensure fair play and justice for all and that the forces with vested interests do not create hardship for the masses.*[116]

---

[116] *idem* [my emphasis]

PART THREE – Business Law Under Islam

Contracts

Under Islamic law, people's property is considered to be as sacred and as inviolable as their life and honour. Shari'ah therefore forbids the "…unlawful devouring of others' property by way of theft, embezzlement, usurpation, bribery, cheating…"[117] and any other dishonest means of acquiring wealth.

Any contracts that do not conform to the tenets of Shari'ah (including, of course, the previously discussed prohibitions on Riba, Gharar etc) are, quite simply, invalid.

As the purpose of writing a contract is to ensure the legal transfer of ownership of goods or usufruct from one party to another, it is important to carefully define some of the terms that will be used.

Wealth

Wealth is considered to be anything that is useable and has legal and material value for people. So from an Islamic legal perspective, something that is considered wealth needs to have value, it needs to be something that we can take possession of and it needs to have a legitimate use. In the Shari'ah sense, anything that is Haram cannot, necessarily, be an item representing wealth to a Muslim.

Property

Property is called Mal and under Islamic commercial law it is, like under Western law, divided in to movable and immovable property. Immovable property usually refers to something that we cannot take away with us, for example, a house.

Property is also either determinate or non-determinate. An item in a contract is determinate ('Ain) if it refers to an actual example of a specific kind. For example, a car with a specific Vehicle Identification Number[118] would be a determinate form of property; we can point out the actual car that is owned and that can be exchanged in a contract. A non-determinate property (Dayn) may be something such as olive oil. We can specify an amount of oil to be exchanged but not the specific molecules making up the oil.

Fungible items can be exchanged one for another, for example, a barrel of one type of crude oil for a barrel of the same type. Different commodities (for example, oil compared to dates) are not fungible with respect to each other.

---

[117] Ayub *op cit* p 101
[118] The Vehicle Identification Number is an ISO standard, modified in some regions, that identifies one specific vehicle at the moment it is constructed. The ISO standard is 3779 and currently comprises 17 alphanumeric characters.

Usufruct

Usufruct is the right to use and to gain profit from the use of some property **without necessarily being the owner of that property**. This is most commonly encountered in leasing of property or the leasing of expensive equipment such as railway carriages by railway companies and aircraft by airlines. The ownership remains with the leaser but the right to gain profit from the leased property (a building, a motor vehicle or other equipment) is with the lessor as long as the lessor pays the required rent for the period of the lease. The use of lease contracts (called Ijarah) is one of the commonest ways in which Islamic banks earn a profit. They gain from the rent collected on property or equipment they own while accepting the normal risks of ownership (maintenance, repair and even replacement).

Ownership

Ownership under Shari'ah falls under one of the following categories:
- Ownership of the Asset itself (Milk ul'Ain)
- Ownership of debt (Milk ud Dayn)
- Ownership of usufruct (Milk ul Manf'at)

Milk ul'Ain is definite and does not relate to time. If someone owns an asset through purchase or succession, the asset's future is entirely at the owner's discretion. Ownership cannot be removed or ignored; it can be transferred at the owner's free will using any of valid (legal) contract forms. If an item is bought on credit, then the item is owned by the buyer at the time that the contract is agreed. The seller has no jurisdiction to retake ownership and can only ask for the payment of the debt to be made. Charges added for late payment are Riba and cannot be added after the contract has been agreed.

Arabic Terms Used in Law of Contract

As the Koran and Sounna taken together form the basis of Islamic law the language of contracts and the subtleties of their interpretation hinge on the use of a number of Arabic terms. Three of the most important terms are:
- Mithaq
- 'Ahd or W'adah
- 'Aqd

Mithaq

Mithaq is more a term relating to contracts in the religious and social domains. They are considered to have a greater sanctity than 'ordinary' contracts. They are mentioned in several verses of the Quran, perhaps the most important of which refers to God's covenant with human beings (13:20-23):

> **Those who fulfill the covenant of Allah and do not break the contract,**
>
> **And those who join that which Allah has ordered to be joined and fear their Lord and are afraid of the evil of [their] account,**

> And those who are patient, seeking the countenance of their Lord,
> and establish prayer and spend from what We have provided for
> them secretly and publicly and prevent evil with good - those will
> have the good consequence of [this] home -
>
> Gardens of perpetual residence; they will enter them with
> whoever were righteous among their fathers, their spouses and
> their descendants. And the angels will enter upon them from
> every gate...[119]

'Ahd

'Ahd (W'adah) in the Fiqh literature) is a unilateral (occasionally bilateral)
promise or commitment. In the Quran (17:34) we find:

> And fulfill [every] commitment. Indeed, the commitment is ever
> [that about which one will be] questioned[120]

'Aqd

The word 'Aqd is synonymous with contract which can be defined as "a legal
relationship created by the conjunction of two declarations, from which flow
legal consequences with regard to the subject matter".[121]   There is an
obligation arising out of mutual agreement. The 'Aqd is:

> 'Aqd (contract) is the most crucial tool for Islamic
> banks...They enter into Amanah, Qard (loan), Shirkah, or
> Wakalah contracts with savers or depositors and Bai', Ijarah,
> Ujrah, Shirkah, Wakalah, Kafalah, Ju'alah and Hawalah
> contracts with those who avail themselves of the financing
> facility from them.[122]

The Derivation of Shari'ah from the Quran and Sounna

Despite the image of Shari'ah in the Western media, there is a considerable
degree of liberty given to the jurists looking for solutions to problems and
issues arising in economic and financial transactions and how Muslims carry
out business dealings. This freedom to interpret derives from:

> ...the methodology of the Shari'ah in dealing with Ibadat
> (devotional acts) and Mu'amalat (transactions). Ibadat are
> held to be universal truths that are unaffected by time and
> space. The Mu'amalat are matters pertaining to individuals
> interacting among themselves. They may change with changes
> in time and space. Imam Ibn Taymiyah explains the difference
> between Ibadat and Mu'amalat in the following words: "The
> acts and deeds of individuals are of two types: Ibadat, whereby
> their religiousness is improved, and Adat or Mu'amalat
> (transactions), which they need in their worldly matters. An

[119] http://quran.com/13 accessed 27 May 2013
[120] http://quran.com/17 accessed 27 May 2013
[121] Ayub op cit p 104
[122] ibid p 105

*inductive survey[123] of the sources of the Shari'ah establishes that devotional acts are sanctioned by express injunctions of the Shari'ah. Thus, **what is not commanded cannot be made obligatory. As regards transactions, the principle governing them would be permissibility and absence of prohibition**. So nothing can be prohibited unless it is proscribed by Allah (SWT) and His Prophet (pbuh) in the overall framework.[124]*

Clearly, Islamic Finance derives from Mu'amalat (transactions) that is those human activities related to production, exchange and distribution of economic wealth. Within this context, income is generated:

"...either through production of goods or providing services by way of sale of goods, their usufruct or expertise. Businesses are conducted in various structures like that of sole proprietorship, partnership (Shirkah), agency (Wakalah) or labour (Ujrah) or forms like sale and lease. All such activities are subject to the observance of certain rules, making the transactions valid and legally enforceable. These rules together constitute the Islamic law of contracts[125].

Contracts should be Written Down

As the Prophet was himself a trader, the Quran's instructions are clear on the subject of contracts. All contracts - barring immediate (on-the-spot) transactions - between people should be written down. This is a surprising demand set against a social background where few people were literate. It is perhaps more so in foreseeing possible difficulties arising there is a default:

"...when you contract a debt for a specified term, write it down. And let a scribe write [it] between you in justice. Let no scribe refuse to write as Allah has taught him. So let him write and let the one who has the obligation dictate. And let him fear Allah, his Lord, and not leave anything out of it. But if the one who has the obligation is of limited understanding or weak or unable to dictate himself, then let his guardian dictate in justice. And bring to witness two witnesses from among your men...And do not be [too] weary to write it, whether it is small or large, for its [specified] term. That is more just in the sight of Allah and stronger as evidence and more likely to prevent doubt between you, except when it is an immediate transaction which you conduct among yourselves[126]..."

The Muslim economic system is at its base a form of free enterprise in that each person is free to pursue his own economic activity. The main difference is that the regulations are based on a religious perspective expressed through *Shari'ah*. Any activity that HARMS either business partner is *haram* under

---

[123] An inductive survey analyses an entire set of writings (or other data) without a specific thesis, the aim of which is to see if any patterns emerge

[124] *idem* [my emphasis]

[125] *idem*

[126] Quran, sura 2 (282)

Shari'ah and the validity of any contract requires that it is motivated by the requirements of *Shari'ah*. In any business transaction there must be the desire to earn *halal* income and all trade must be through mutual consent only – a sale through any form of coercion is *haram* and invalid.[127]

Any and all contracts that, for example, promote immorality or run counter to public policy or try to sell the property of a third party are deemed to be void.

There are several slightly different opinions on what is required for a valid contract but they differ only in small details. For example, Iqbal[128] considers the following aspects important for valid contracts under Islamic law[129].

1. Freedom to determine the conditions of the contract
2. Conscious agreement within the *Shari'ah* framework
3. Prohibition on taking property from others without compensation
4. Mutual Profit (equality in reciprocal engagements)
5. Prohibition on *riba* and *gharar* (games included)
6. Attribution of profit in line with risk taken
7. Maximum information available to both contracting parties
8. Avoidance of negative effects on the lives of others and society in general
9. Prohibition on asymmetric contracts containing special clauses etc
10. Respect for the letter and the spirit of the contract

Establishing a Contract

A contract requires: two parties capable (that is, mature and sane) of entering into a contract; an offer (Ijab) and acceptance (Qabul); a legal form (Sharie) for the union between the two declarations (offer and acceptance) and the contract must be free from all prohibiting elements. Ayub uses Sanhuri's seven components[130] to illustrate a good basis for the establishment of a contract:

- the concurrence of offer and acceptance;
- the unity of the Majlis (session/meeting) of a contract;
- plurality of the contracting parties;
- sanity or the power of distinction of the contracting parties;
- subject matter susceptible to delivery;

---

[127] There is an interesting discussion on adhesion (standard form) contracts in the video quoted above starting at 24mins. This stems from the fact that there is no free choice in some of these contracts eg for monopolistic utility contracts. Under Shari'ah these contracts have been declared halal as they have the benefits of saving time, being cost-effective and ensuring that everyone is treated in the same way. It would also be impractical and prohibitively expensive to negotiate individual contracts in this context

[128] Iqbal M (2007), A Guide to Islamic Finance, Risk Books

[129] I have taken this from Causse-Broquet *op cit* p42 "10 Commandments to Obey according to Iqbal". My translation from French

[130] Ayub *op cit* p 106

- the object (Mahall) defined;
- the beneficial nature of the object, in that trade in it is permitted as per Shari'ah rules

Offer and Acceptance

The first of these seven components, the offer and acceptance:

> ...is the procedure or the means by which a contract is made. Juristic rules require that the offer should be in clear language and [it must be] unconditional. There should be conformity of the offer and acceptance on the subject matter and the consideration and [the] issuance of the offer and its acceptance should be in the same session...An offer (Ijab) is the necessary condition of a valid contract. It has been defined as a declaration or a firm proposal made first with a view to creating an obligation, while the subsequent declaration is termed acceptance (Qabul). Ijab signifies the willingness of a party to do something positive.[131]

Unity of Session

The session, or Majlis, is the period during which the contracting parties are negotiating. Shari'ah requires that acceptance should conform to the offer and should be made in the same meeting. This is derived from Sounna of the Prophet: "The contracting parties have the right of option (to finalize or not) until they separate".[132] Of course, this definition is impractical if the subject matter is a modern complex project involving governments and large companies. This is well illustrated by a decision of the Federal Shariat Court (FSC) of Pakistan:

> "A narrow interpretation of Majlis would mean that the offer of the promisor should be accepted without any delay and without giving the promisee any opportunity to think or consult someone in order to make up his mind. This may be practicable in small transactions but will fail in bigger transactions, which may require considerable inquiry. Thus, if an offer is made for sale of a factory, it will require inquiry into the title, power to sell, value of machinery, value of building, its liabilities, if any, profitability, etc. If the Majlis is interpreted to mean a single session, no one will consider purchasing a property... "[133]

It is now accepted by most jurists that the Majlis, in as much as it refers to a single meeting, is no more than a convenient way of representing the entire negotiation that occurs between the contracting parties. Whatever time is taken by the promise to communicate his acceptance may be called a continuance of the same meeting.

---

[131] *idem* [However, a contract may require that someone abstains from doing something]
[132] Bukhari, Sahih, Kitab al Buyu quoted in Ayub *op cit* p 107
[133] FSC of Pakistan quoted in Ayub *op cit* p107

Plurality of the Contracting Parties

It may seem obvious, but there must be genuine buyers and a seller for the contract to be a valid one. That is important in a market auction scenario where certain "buyers" may be acting on behalf of the seller to push the price of the subject matter up. Any sale that has been contracted in this situation is void and the buyer (assuming he comes to know about the manipulation) can demand a refund of all monies for return of the goods bought.

Sanity or Power of Distinction of the Contracting Parties

Those who are not capable of understanding the nature of the market or the legal nature of a sale, whether they are under a legal age or perhaps have a low educational attainment, are not permitted to engage in a contract to buy or sell.

Subject Matter of the Contract

Under Shari'ah, the contractual obligation of one party is the consideration[134] for the contractual obligation of the other party. The subject matter will depend on the type of contract that is being entered into but, in general, the subject must:

- Exist or be capable of creation
- Have value
- Be usable
- Be something that can be owned or its title must be transferable
- Be able to be delivered/possessed
- Specified
- Quantified
- Belong to the seller

Subject Matter Deliverable

If a non-existent thing is sold, even with the consent of both parties, that sale is void under Shari'ah. This means that the sale of debt and all short-selling practices on the stock market are prohibited. There are certain contracts for non-existent items that are permissible because they are tightly specified and include objects made to order in a factory. These are discussed under the contract type called Salam.

Beneficial Trade

The items for sale must not include anything prohibited in the Quran, for example, alcohol, pork or intoxicants. Neither must the purpose of the contract be contrary to the objectives of Shari'ah, for example, running a brothel or a gambling house.

Under Shari'ah it is not permitted to sell something that is not owned by the seller and, in addition, the item to be sold cannot be the subject of a legal

---

[134] The consideration is something given in return – it isn't necessarily money

charge such as a mortgage or secured loan. The lien must be lifted before the item can be sold.

Subject Matter must be Clearly Defined

The consideration for the subject matter must be agreed **and fixed** at the time that the contract is executed. If the price is not clear then the contract is void. Additionally, the exact units that are used, both for measuring the item(s) for sale and the units used to pay for the item must be clearly specified in the contract.

The final step is that it must be clear exactly when the contract is struck. This may be through a handshake a nod of the head or something more formal such as a signature. At this point the ownership of the item, along with all of its associated risks is passed to the buyer who must pay the price agreed either immediately or on a clearly specified date in the future in the case of a credit sale. Regardless of whether or not money has passed hands ownership will have been transferred and no additional charges can be added to the price, even if the buyer is late making the payment as required. The addition of a known amount of "penalty", even for late payment, is considered Riba under Shari'ah and that is entirely forbidden.

With the basics in place, we can now move on to a discussion of the different types of contract that occur under Islamic Finance.

Types of Contract

Shari'ah jurists, (following the Hanbali tradition) break contracts down into valid (Sahih), voidable/defective (Fasid) and void (Batil). Any contract where one of the conditions for legality is missing will make the contract invalid.

> *The validity of any contract depends on the legality or illegality of the subject matter, the existence and precise determination of the subject matter, delivery or the ability to deliver the subject matter without involvement of excessive uncertainty and precise determination of the price or consideration in a contract. A valid contract is one which is in accordance with Islamic law, both as regards its 'Asl (fundamental components, nature or essence) and Wasf (accessory circumstances or external attributes). A contract is deemed valid when all elements of the contract (form or offer and acceptance, the subject matter and the contracting parties) are found to be in order; the conditions of each element have been met and it is free from external prohibited activities like Riba, Gharar, etc.*[135]

---

[135] Ayub *op cit* p118

Nafiz and Mawquf

Contracts may also be effective immediately (Nafiz) or at a future date (Mawquf). A *mawquf* contract becomes *nafiz* immediately upon lifting the cause of suspension. This type of suspension is used in the contract types called Ijarah (leasing) and Istisna'a (manufacturing to order) as the buyer does not own the usufructs of the 'purchased' item until he takes physical possession of it. In these contracts the suspension is a planned part of the contract.

A contract may also be suspended for other reasons among which are: inability on the part of one of the parties or lack of authority in one of the parties. Inability may be due to the age of one of the parties or the ability of one of the parties to make competent decisions, for example, due to educational attainment. Lack of authority may mean that the seller does not possess the items to be sold or the right to sell the items on the part of a third party.

Valid Binding and Valid Non-Binding Contracts

It is legal to write contracts that are non-binding. A binding (lazim) contract is one in which neither of the parties to the contract can unilaterally revoke the contract unless both parties agree to an option to do this. A non-binding contract gives either of the parties the right to revoke the contract without the consent of the other. This type of contract is called Ghair Lazim. There are two practical reasons for the existence of such contracts:

- The nature of the contract, for example where both parties are allowed to revoke independently, such as in an agency relationship or partnership in business
- An option is included to allow a transfer of ownership or responsibility, for example, the ownership of shares can be transferred by a shareholder without reference to the company whose shares they are

Voidable (Fasid) Contracts

A contract that has all the elements of a valid contract but requires an exchange of prohibited items or services will not necessarily be void; rather it will be voidable. If the subject matter causing the problem can be removed or brought into line with Shari'ah requirements then the voidable contract can be declared valid. There are two types of invalidity:

- Intrinsic causes which relate to the basic elements of the contract, such as unlawfulness or nonexistence of the subject matter, or the absence of contractual capacity in any of the parties.
- Extrinsic causes that relate to Wasf, i.e. external attributes such as Riba or Gharar contained in the contract.[136]

---

[136] Ayub *op cit* p 120

Other factors that might lead to a contract being unenforceable (ie irregular or voidable) include:

- Defective consent – eg coercion
- A lack of value-relevant information – eg deferred pricing
- A benefit accruing to one party at the expense of the other

Void (Batil) Contracts

The nature of a void contract is clearly described by Mansoori in Ayub's book:

> *Contracts that do not fulfil the conditions relating to offer and acceptance, subject matter, consideration and possession or delivery, or involve some illegal external attributes are considered void (Batil). In other words, if major conditions relating to the form of the contract (acceptance does not conform to the offer, or the offer does not exist at the time of acceptance, etc.), parties to the contract (sane and mature), possession and deliverability of the subject matter are not fulfilled, the contract is Batil.*[137]

A *Batil* contract does not have any effect. There is no change of title, the seller cannot have the consideration and the transaction will be null and void.

Some Contracts Involve Compensation, Others Not

Not all contracts are receive compensation under Islamic Law. These contracts are classified as non-commutative. There are several non-commutative contract types:

- Hibah – Gift
- Wasiyyah – bequest
- Waqf – endowment
- Kafalah – guarantee
- 'Ariyah (loan of a usable item free of charge)
- Qard (Loan)
- Hawalah (assignment of debt)

These contracts also differ in their treatment of void conditions; they do not become void; the void condition becomes ineffective. As an example, if someone borrows money at interest, the requirement to pay interest is void. However, the requirement to pay back the principal amount remains a legal requirement.

The commutative contract types break down into those relating to the object and those that describe how the price has been defined. Contracts classified by object include:

- Bai' Muqayadhah (barter sale)
- Bai' al Hal (simultaneous exchange of goods for money)

---

[137] *ibid* p 123

- Bai' al Sarf (exchange of money or monetary units)
- Bai' Salam (sale - immediate payment and deferred delivery)
- Bai' Mu'ajjal (sale - deferred payment or credit sale)
- Bai' Mutlaq (sale of goods for money, also called absolute sale)

Contracts classified by price definition:

- Bai' Tawliyah (resale at cost price)
- Bai' Murabahah (resale at cost price plus profit)
- Bai' Wadhi'ah (resale with loss)
- Bai' Musawamah (sale without reference to the original cost)

There are contracts relating to the hiring of services and things:

- Ijarat al Ashkas (rendering services)
- Ijarat al Ashya (letting things)

A manufacturing contract is called Istisna'a and a contract for agency (which may be remunerated or not) is called Wakalah. Finally, conditional contracts are those that depend on some future event occurring or he passage of time. In general, these are considered less preferable contracts but there are cases where the stipulation of some condition may be unavoidable (for example a guarantee of repair work for faulty manufacture). The aim would be to ensure that neither party gains an advantage over the other one as a result of the condition being enforced.

The overall purpose of all the conditions, written or spoken, placed into contracts is to ensure that transactions are fair. As Ayub puts it:

> *The Islamic system disapproves of any exploitation or injustice on the part of any of the parties involved. To achieve this objective, the Sharl'ah has advised some prohibitions and recommended some ethics. Detailed study of the rules and norms reveals that Islamic finance is, in essence, an ethical system and ethics need to be an inseparable part of the system. What is not prohibited is permissible. Therefore, all contracts are valid unless they violate the text of the Holy Qur'¯an or Sunnah of the holy Prophet (pbuh), or are in conflict with the objectives of the Shari'ah.*[138]

Summary

To ensure that transactions are ethical, valid contracts must comprise the following:

- The [correct] form, i.e. offer and acceptance, which can be conveyed by spoken words, in writing or through

---

[138] Ayub *op cit* p127

indication and conduct. The acceptance should conform to the offer in all its details

• Contracting parties, who must have the capacity for execution

• Subject matter, which must be lawful, in existence at the time of the contract and should be capable of being delivered and precisely determined either by description or by inspection[139]

Later chapters will discuss the main contract forms in more detail.

---

[139] *ibid* p 128 [adapted slightly from the basic text]

Islamic Commercial Law and Trading

Under Shari'ah both society and individuals are encouraged to increase their wealth. This growth takes place through the production of goods and exchange of values among parties in the market. Shari'ah does not limit profits or fix prices; rather it promotes the free flow of goods in an open market environment. Shari'ah does require, however, the avoidance of Riba and Gharar and the fulfilment of certain rules of business to ensure that:

> **"...the (wealth) does not make a circuit between the wealthy among you" (Quran 59:7)[140]**

This means that Islamic banks have to operate on the basis of profit and not interest. This profit comes from three main areas:

- Trading
- Leasing
- Profit and Loss (PLS) contracts

Bai' - Exchange of Value

The literal meaning of 'Bai is the exchange of one thing for another. Different exchanges involve different rules with respect to the liabilities and benefits for the parties involved in the exchange. Trade involves the reciprocal exchange of property with its rights and usufruct. Ijarah, which is the sale of usufruct, the lessor gives the lessee the right to the usufruct but retains ownership and the risks associated with ownership. A loan is a temporary but complete transfer of ownership (along with the usufruct) to the borrower. The user can use the item as if it was one of his own, but he has to return it to the owner at the specified time. The final type of 'Bai is called Shirkah which is the sharing of both the ownership and the profit or loss among partners.

Trade and Riba

In a trading transaction, there is, "the transfer of complete and instant ownership that is irreversible once finalized."[141] It is permitted to delay the delivery of one of the items in the trade only if the genera of the exchanged items are different - so wheat can be delivered at a later date if it has been paid for in money. However, wheat and barley, which are of the same genus, must be exchanged on the spot or the trade would be Riba. This is because one of the traders now holds twice what he held before the trade took place and the other has nothing. This is an unjust transaction that is not permitted under Shari'ah.

> **"And Allah has permitted trade and prohibited Riba"[142]**

The consequence is that you cannot trade in money, because all currencies are of the same genus.

---

[140] Quran sura 59:7 quoted in Ayub *op cit* p 129

[141] Ayub *op cit* p 131

[142] Quran Sura 2:275

This has consequences for how banks operate within an Islamic context. They are required under Shari'ah to make a profit from trade and related activities without charging interest or certainly without using contractual devices to cover up activities that attract interest based solely on time. This is because in a riba-based business, reward (in the form of money paid in interest) is guaranteed to one party while leaving the risk entirely with the other party. This ignores the important Shari'ah principle of Al-Kharaj bi-al-Daman which means that one can claim a profit only if one is willing to bear the liability also.

Truthful Merchants are ranked with the Prophets

The respected position of Bai' in an Islamic economy is emphasised by the Prophet as illustrated by Ayub:

> The holy Prophet also said: "The best earnings are those of the businessman who does not tell a lie when he speaks; does not misappropriate the trust; does not break the word if he promises; does not cavil while making purchases; does not boast while selling his goods; does not prolong the period of repayment of loan; and does not cause difficulty to his debtors!" Further: "The best type of earning is Bai' [that is] based on truth and earnings of one by his own hands"[143]

Approved Forms of Bai'

Within the Shari'ah context there is a lot of emphasis placed on the beneficial nature of trade. Trade is, therefore to be carried out in approved forms and under clear conditions:

> The approved forms of Bai' reflect the main principles of mutual consent of the parties and justice, with an emphasis on good manners, leniency and honesty. Mutual consent can exist only when there is volition, truthfulness as against coercion, fraud and lying. Justice includes imperatives like fulfilment of promise and contracts, correct weights and measures, clear and definite stipulation of price, nature and amount of work, wages and payments, honesty and sincerity. Good manners prescribed by the Shari'ahin conducting any business include politeness, forgiveness, due compensation and removal of hardship faced by others.[144]

The Object of the Sale

The object of a sale must exist or be easily creatable according to detailed specifications and:

> ...the object must be pure, lawful (Mubah), clean, wholesome... marketable and bearing legal value. It must be Mal-e-

---

[143] Ayub op cit p 132
[144] ibid p 134

> *Mutaqawam (wealth having a commercial value); its underlying cause (Sabab) must be lawful, and it must not be proscribed by Islamic law; ... the object must be in existence at the time of the contract and the vendor must be the real owner of the commodity to be sold.*[145]

This means that a vendor (such as a car salesman in a showroom) cannot sell a car until he has taken possession of it and that the car is, at least, in his constructive possession.[146] The aim, quite simply, is to avoid Gharar – perhaps about the quality of the car or its availability.

Prices and Profit Margin

Prices and profit margins are not fixed in Shari'ah. These should be settled by the forces of supply and demand. There is, however, an important role for the state in ensuring that certain moral, religious and cultural norms are met. For example:

> *The Shari'ah does not allow excessive profiteering (Ghaban-e-Fahish), which means that [if] a person sells a commodity stating explicitly or giving the impression that he is charging the market price, when actually he is charging an exorbitant price, taking benefit from the ignorance of the purchaser. If the purchaser comes to know afterwards that he has been charged excessively, he has the option to rescind the contract and take back his money*[147]

The profit margin, inferring from several sources, should not deviate much from the following norms:

- Wares – 5%
- Animals – 10 %
- Real Estate – 20%

Cash and Credit Sales

The practice of buying and selling on credit is an old one that was widespread in the "Golden Age of Islam" before approximately 1100 CE (493 AH). In the opinion of the jurists, the seller is free to indicate two prices; one for cash and the other for credit. The price, once accepted by the buyer, is fixed when the contract is struck. The buyer uses cash or credit appropriately. The seller, to avoid charges of Riba and Ghaban-e-Fahish, must be able to show that the credit price proposed is in accordance with current practice in the market.

This practice is, perhaps, open to charges of Riba. It has been the subject of much discussion among jurists of all schools and the majority opinion is that

---

[145] *ibid* p 135

[146] Constructive possession means that the car could be in a garage to which the owner has access and from which the purchaser can collect the car without any delay following the contract of sale.

[147] Ayub *op cit* p 139

as long as the price is settled (ie cash sale accepted or credit sale accepted) it is entirely a matter for the traders as to the price to be paid. However, the agreement to take cash or credit must be made before the end of the trading session. Ayub quotes several juristic opinions, for example:

> *According to Tirmidhi, some jurists have explained this in the sense that a person states: "I sell this cloth for cash for 10 and on credit for 20 (dirhams)" and at separation, one price is not settled. If one of the two prices is settled, it is not prohibited. Tohfatul Ahwazi, Sharah Jam'i al Tirmidhi, explains that if the seller says that he sells the cloth for 10 for cash and 20 on credit, and the buyer accepts either of the two prices; or if a buyer says that he purchases for 20 on credit or the parties separate having settled on any of the prices, the sale will be valid[148]*

Uncertainty Is Prohibited

This has already been discussed earlier but warrants emphasis. Contracts must be free from uncertainty about the subject matter and its counter value in exchanges. As business risk is a part of life, the prohibition on Gharar leads to the:

> *...requirement...that the commodity must be defined, determined and deliverable and clearly known to the contracting parties; quality and quantity must be stipulated; the contract must not be doubtful or uncertain so far as the rights and obligations of the contracting parties are concerned and the parties should know the actual state of the goods[149]*

This has a particular implication with some practices that are common in modern stock markets, foreign exchange markets and the market for the type of insurance against risk known as credit default swaps. All of these markets have mechanisms for profit that result directly from the presence of gharar. These markets even allow untrained members of the public (who are often taken as no more than marks) to borrow large sums of money at interest to be able to take part in trades. Similarly, there is a trade in oil, wheat, orange juice and a range of other commodities where a trader "purchases" some commodity with the sole purpose of speculating on a higher price – without the intention of ever taking actual possession of the commodities in question. All Shari'ah committees have declared such transactions to be prohibited as they involve Riba (money borrowed at interest to purchase options) and Gharar (the market could go either way based on unknowable future events or even brute manipulation by powerful "players" in the market). Finally these markets involve the sale of goods that are not in the possession of the vendor.

---

[148] *ibid* p 141
[149] *ibid* p 143

Conditional Sales Are Not Permitted

Islamic law does not approve sales that are conditional on other events that may or may not occur. This introduces uncertainty into the sales contact which is forbidden under Shari'ah. Ayub illustrates this point as follows:

> ...a person says to another: "I will sell you this house if any third person sells me his house". Gharar in this transaction pertains to the time of the meeting, the condition and finalization of the contract. Conditions of gift, marriage, Qard [loan] or Shirkah [partnership] as a part of a sale contract render it a prohibited contract from the Shari'ah angle[150]

There is a difference of opinion among jurists with a new consensus forming around the teachings of Ibn Taymiyah who "rejects only those conditions which contradict a clear provision of the Quran, the Sunnah, the scholarly consensus or act to contradict the object of the contract."[151] Ibn Taymiyah objects only to the combination of onerous and gratuitous contracts such as loan (Qard) and sale since this type of condition can lead to hidden compensation for the loan and hence to charges of Riba and Gharar. The conditions, however, can be combined informally, as in the case of Tawarruq. In Tawarruq, a needy person buys something on credit and sells it immediately, in a separate transaction, for cash. This has been declared legitimate by most scholars as it is practically impossible to police this sort of behaviour only to express a moral disapproval of it. Tawarruq has been declared Makrooh (reprehensible) in the opinion of some of the eminent jurists.

Deposit Sales – Bai' Al'arbun

Paying for something on deposit and then making the second payment on collection is a legitimate transaction. However, there is no real consensus about what to do when the depositor does not collect the object of the sale and does not, therefore, complete the sale. Does the vendor have the right to confiscate the deposit? The answer is not definitive. Ayub comments that:

> ...in cases of involvement of absolute Gharar or injustice with the buyer (when he committed to purchase, but cannot do so due to any unforeseen happening), downpayment confiscation might not be permissible. However, to the extent of a customary practice wherein parties do business in the market with free consent and any unforeseen events are also taken into account, it would be permissible on the basis of 'Urf. The Islamic Fiqh Council of the OIC and the AAOIFI have also allowed customary downpayment sale with the condition that a time limit is specified.[152]

---

[150] ibid p 144
[151] ibid p 145
[152] ibid p 146

Sale of Debt - Bai' Al Dayn

If a transaction involves the purchase of an object on credit, the note of credit signed by the buyer CANNOT be sold on. This is due to rules on Riba and Gharar. The person who would buy the debt does not have access to the original debtor (who has signed a contract with someone else) so there is an element of uncontrollable risk (gharar) present. If the debt is passed on at a discount then Riba is involved as money has increased in value for the buyer by the passage only of time.

This means that promissory notes, bills of exchange or export bills cannot be treated in the same way by an Islamic bank as a conventional bank. The OIC Fiqh Academy and the Shari'ah scholar consensus consider the sale or purchase of securities or documents representing debt at a price other than its face value to be incompatible with Shari'ah. Even when presented at face value, the sale of debt is permitted only when the buyer has access to the original debtor, as in Hawallah. Hawallah is where a person agrees to take on someone's debt with the express intention of paying it back to the creditor in line with the original contract. As securitisation of future income streams is a common method by which companies raise cash for new projects through the intervention of financial institutions, this restriction means that Islamic banks have to find different ways to make profits in a competitive world. Shari'ah compliant securitisation is available as will be described in a later chapter.

Use of Ruses (Hiyal)

Legal Fictions to Circumvent Shari'ah Restrictions

Many attempts have been made to legally circumvent various prohibitions on, for example, Riba. The technical legality of Hiyal is not in doubt. Hiyal involves the use of procedural devices that show people how to avoid 'clashes with the law' without avoiding the law. It does, however, runs counter to the spirit of Shari'ah as expressed by Mahmasani in Ayub:

> First – the Shari'ah texts are not aimed at the deeds themselves but rather at the interest which those deeds are intended to serve. Therefore, all acts should be interpreted in the light of their spirit and intent and not by their appearances...

> Second – attempts at bypassing the law are tantamount to deceit, and deceit is prohibited in Shari'ah as evidenced by the Qur'an and the Sunnah...

> Third – the Prophet, the Companions and the Followers have been quoted in opposition to legal fictions...

> Ibn Masud and Ibn Abbas, following the example of the Prophet, were reported to have ruled against acceptance of a gift from the debtor before settlement of the debt, because the purpose of a gift under such circumstances was the postponement of payment of the debt and a ruse to legalize interest. Similarly, Muslim jurists, their followers and the

doctors of traditions such as Imam Bukhari agreed on the prohibition of legal fictions and on the necessity of avoiding them"[153]

An example of Hiyal, known as Bai' al 'Inah, takes the form of a double sale called a buy-back. It acts to cover up the sale of a loan at interest.

*...a ruser sells a commodity of $1000 payable after a year and then buys the same commodity for $950 on cash payment, has been declared unlawful due to the involvement of the element of Riba. This practice is known as Bai' al 'Inah, defined as a double sale involving "buy-back", by which the borrower and the lender sell and then resell a commodity between them, once for cash and once for a higher price on credit, with the net result of a loan with interest. **Jurists consider 'Inah a stratagem whose function is to attain illegal ends through legal means.** Ibn Qudama says: "If a person sells something on credit, it is not permissible to buy that commodity at a price less than the price at which he sold.[154]*

This has implications for the Islamic equivalent of a mortgage called a Diminishing Musharakah, whereby a bank purchases part-ownership in a plot of land or a building and the client **promises** to repurchase this after an agreed amount of time. The time period has to long enough to avoid charges of Bai' al 'Inah arising from this sale and buy-back arrangement. More details are in the chapter on Islamic Mortgages.

The Option to Annul a Contract (Khiyar)

If a buyer is not happy with the sale there is, if the sale can be shown to be void, the right to return goods and the seller must return the consideration that was exchanged. However, there are cases where the right to exercise such an option is not automatic. This is covered by the Islamic doctrine of option called Khiyar and must be stipulated in the contract if the option of return is required. There are five types of Khiyar option (this use of the word option is not to be confused with the concept of options involved in the derivatives markets)[155]:

- Khiyar al-Shart: a stipulation that any of the parties has the option to rescind the sale within so many (specified) days; this is also termed Bai' al Khiyar
- Khiyar al Ro'yat: an option to be exercised on inspecting the goods [which, if they do not meet the terms of the]...contract, can be returned after inspection if such an option has been provided for in the sale agreement
- Khiyar al 'Aib: an option with regard to defect – goods can be returned if found to be defective; this kind of option is

---

[153] *ibid* p 148
[154] *idem* My emphasis
[155] *ibid* p 151 My clarifications in square brackets

available even if no such condition is stipulated in the contract if the defect was not brought to the notice of the buyer at the time of the contract and the defect caused a visible decrease in the value of the sold commodity. However, if the seller declares at the time of the contract that he will not be held responsible for any defect in the commodity, the contract is valid according to [the]Hanafis

- Khiyar al Wasf: the option of quality – where goods are sold by specified quality, but that quality is absent, the goods can be returned
- Khiyar-e-Ghaban: the option relating to price – where goods are sold at a price far higher than the market price, and the client is told or given the impression that he has been charged the market price

As always there are exceptions that prevent Khiyar options being included in the contract. For example, under Salam and Istisna'a, Khiyar al Ro'yat is not available if the goods have been delivered according to specifications.

Loan and Debt under Commercial Shari'ah

In Shari'ah lending is a virtuous act. That is, lenders cannot receive compensation for the use of the loaned object, be it money, gold, dates or, perhaps, a lawn mower. The lender is obliged to give back the loaned item or, in the case of money, to repay the loaned amount in an agreed timeframe. Any demand for an excess over the loaned amount is Riba – it is completely forbidden under Shari'ah. Between individuals, there should not even be a penalty clause in any agreement relating to a loan. However, the Shari'ah boards of Islamic banks (with the intention to include moral hazard for delinquent lenders) do permit the bank (as a public institution) to charge delinquency fees, which must then be donated to charity.

It is practically impossible to avoid debt-creation in a business environment. Whether this is through the offer, for example, of credit facilities or by the act of forming a partnership to trade, there is always an obligation to repay someone. The differences between different types of obligations created in business were recognised in the Quran and clarified over time in Hadith and Fiqh. When discussing, debt the important terms...

> ...are Qard, Salaf and Dayn. While the former two terms relate to the giving or taking of loans, Dayn comes into existence as a result of any other contract or credit transaction...Legally, Qard means to give anything having value in the ownership of any other **by way of virtue** so that the latter can [use it] for his benefit with the condition that the same or similar amount of that thing should be paid back on demand or at the settled time.[156]

Qard is a subset of Salaf (which is itself cognate with Salam). A loan is Qard if it is payable on demand. A loan is Salaf if it has a fixed time frame for payment.

Interest on Loans and Debt Is Prohibited

The charging of interest was a common business profession among the rich at the time of the coming of the Prophet and the perceived injustice has led to its prohibition. This applies to Islamic banks, which as intermediaries in the business environment, will always need to lend money or create debt. Under Shari'ah:

> ...whatever may be their structure; Islamic banks should not be in a position to earn money from money and should be involved in real goods for the purpose of financing. As such, by using trade and lease-based modes/products, they are creating debt and have to abide by the Shari'ah rules relating to Dayn[157]

---

[156] *ibid* p 151 My emphasis
[157] *ibid* p 158

The Quran is also clear that loans and debts need to be witnessed except between parties that trust each other:

> O ye who believe! When ye deal with each other, in lending or transactions involving future obligations for a fixed period of time reduce it to writing. Let a scribe write down faithfully between the parties; let not the scribe refuse to write: as Allah has taught him, so let him write.[158]

Although lending is unavoidable, borrowing for should be for valid purposes and not to fund lavish consumption.[159] Furthermore,

> ...it has to be borne in mind that a loan must be paid. Debt is not forgiven, even for martyrs. Further, a loan whereby something in excess of the principal is exacted becomes unlawful, as it amounts to Riba. There is no exemption on the basis that a Qard transaction has taken place between a Muslim and a non-Muslim, an employer and an employee or a State and the people. Prohibition of Riba means that money can be lent without any expectation of return over the amount of the principal, and as such, every loan that draws forth or stipulates profit is unlawful. The holy Prophet (pbuh) has said that after making a loan, the creditor must even refrain from accepting a present from the borrower unless exchange of such presents was in practice between the borrower and the lender before the advancement of the loan[160]

Duty of a Debtor

Under Shari'ah the duty of a debtor, above all else, is to repay the loan in fulfilment of the promise or contract made with the creditor. A debtor who wilfully enters default is behaving, from a moral and religious perspective, unjustly and there are Hadith recommending that:

> ...a debtor who is able to pay but does not repay the debt can be arrested and embarrassed...and that the greatest sin after Kabair, is to leave, after death, unpaid debt where there is no one to pay the same...In desperate circumstances when the debtor is really unable to pay, he should take the creditor into his confidence and regret his inability to pay the debt. The holy Prophet (pbuh) has warned that a believer's soul remains encumbered with the debt until he pays. He also said that the best among people is he who is the best in payment of his liabilities... The Shari'ah even allows punishment of a debtor who does not pay his debt, and if he defaults wilfully, he can be arrested, punished and dealt with harshly.

---

[158] Holy Quran (2:282)

[159] Which is something that Western banks encourage extensively with loans for holidays, loans for cars etc

[160] *ibid* p 160

The fact that there are a relatively large number of non-performing loans in many countries of the world[161] shows that many borrowers (clearly not all, especially those hit hard by the current global economic crisis) do not take seriously their responsibility to pay their debts while continuing to live beyond their means. Ayub emphasises that, "Islam requires that a debtor should not only pay the debt in time, but also express thanks and pay gratitude to the creditor while repaying the amount. It is also desirable on the part of the authorities to make relevant laws and accounting and auditing standards to minimize the chances of non-payment of loans or other moral hazard threats in present-day societies.[162]"

Advice for Creditors

The Quran encourages creditors to give extra time for the repayment of a loan or even to waive it completely if the debtor is in dire straits. However, the majority of jurists do not allow the arrest or punishment of debtors who are really in financial difficulties. They recommend giving more time to make the repayment. Some jurists, however, advocate the "short, sharp shock of a prison sentence followed up by detailed research into the debtor's actual ability to pay[163].

Loans with a fixed due date cannot be recalled early as long as the debtor meets the terms of the agreement. On the other hand, an extension of time for repayment of the loan is an entirely discretionary act on the part of the creditor. Case histories from early Islamic times suggest that:

> ...even a destitute debtor is not entitled to get more time as his right. He will not be remitted of the repayment of debt and whatever he earns over and above his normal food needs, should go towards repayment of the debt.[164]

Gracious Repayment of a Loan

Repaying a loan in excess of the principal and without a precondition is commendable and compatible with the Shari'ah. However,

> ...gracious repayment of debt is a matter of individual discretion and cannot be adopted as a system, because this would mean that a loan would necessarily yield a profit. All references in the Fiqh literature that we find in favour of gracious payment of debt indicate that addition should not be a precondition, explicit or implicit.[165]

Clearly, banks and other financial institutions under Shari'ah would need to avoid regular grace and favour payments lest it result in an expectation of profit. That would be nothing less than Riba.

---

[161] Since 2000, the average percentage of non-performing loans (more than 90 days overdue) is 5.1%. The trend is down over the last 13 years. The statistics were retrieved from http://data.worldbank.org/indicator/FB.AST.NPER.ZS

[162] Ayub *op cit* p 162

[163] Ayub quotes the example of Abu Hanifa on p 162

[164] *idem*

[165] *ibid* p 163

Bank Account Deposits are Loans (Qard)

An Islamic bank's current account depositors are, in effect, giving the bank an interest free loan. These deposits are deemed as Qard under Shari'ah and must be repaid on demand. As there is no risk to these assets then the depositors are not in a position to profit from their deposits so there is no return for the depositors using this type of account. Islamic banks, however, do have accounts that allow depositors to share in the banks Profit and Loss Sharing (PLS) activities. In these accounts, the depositors indicate their acceptance to put their money at risk (there are different levels of risk available) and make a profit based on the weighted proportion of their money in each venture. This will be discussed in more detail later.

Penalising Default

In the modern era of Islamic Banking, the spectre of default presents a clear and present danger. Ayub is clear that a, "non-performing portfolio and default on the part of clients is a serious problem if...

> ...clients do not honour their commitment in respect of timely payment of a debt created in an instalment sale, Murabahah or leasing, or do not pay the banks' share of profit in participatory modes, or do not deliver goods at the stipulated time in Salam and Istisna'a, it could cause irreparable loss to the system, the banks and financial institutions and ultimately to the savers and the respective economies.[166]

There is clearly a need for a mechanism to reduce the moral hazard of people not being punished in some way for their failure to pay their debts. Consequently (and this only applies to loans classified as Dayn),

> all Shari'ah bodies like the Islamic Fiqh Council of the OIC, the AAOIFI, the Shariat Appellate Bench of the Supreme Court of Pakistan, etc. have approved the provision of penalty clauses embedded in contractual agreements that keep a balance between the requirement in view of the severity of the problem and that of the Shari'ah conditions/principles to keep the fine difference between interest and a Murabahah profit intact. The penalty thus received has to be given to charity.[167]

Insolvency

Ayub gives a brief description of a muflis

> If a debtor [cannot] pay his debt(s), he is...bankrupt (Muflis) in Islamic commercial law. In such cases it must be ensured that the debtor is not resorting to fraudulent bankruptcy, [if he is] he can be pressed and even imprisoned for payment of debt. However, if a person is really in trouble and there is little

---

[166] *ibid* p 165
[167] *ibid* p 166

chance of his ability to pay in the foreseeable future, he can be declared insolvent; all his assets will be sold and the proceeds distributed among the creditors on a pro rata basis. If some of the debts remain unpaid, he must be given time for easement. The State or the regulators of the financial system can play an important role in resolving such issues...[168]

Hawalah – Assignment of Debt

The word Hawalah is the transfer of something from one person to another or from one situation to another. In the legal sense, it is the transfer of debt from one person to another, that is, one debtor replaces another. The Hawalah contract was popular during the early centuries of Islam and was carried to Europe during the crusades of the 12th Century CE. Its importance in the creation of a commercial medium of exchange is described Ayub:

> *The contract of Hawalah, together with the contract of al-Suftajah, formed the basis of [the] bill of exchange in Islamic commercial law. The term "Hawalah" also applies to a mandate to pay and denotes the document by which the transfer of debt is completed. In this sense, it [is] a promissory note or a bill of exchange. A number of products and services provided by the banking industry today are forms of Hawalah, like cheques, drafts, pay orders, remittances, promissory notes, bills of exchange...etc.*

> *The difference between "sale of debt", which is prohibited, and the "assignment of debt", which is permissible, is that, [in assignment], there is recourse to the assignor or the original debtor if the assignee does not pay the debt for any reason. In the sale of debt, the purchaser of the debt instrument has no recourse to the seller of the debt, and therefore, due to the involvement of Gharar and Riba, the sale of debt is prohibited, except in the case where it is subject to the rules of Hawalah.[169]*

The assignee in a Hawalah contract cannot be paid for this service. The contract is a binding one that cannot be unilaterally revoked and if the assignee dies the debt reverts to the original holder. The importance of paying one's debts under Islam derives directly from the reported words of the Prophet:

> *"Procrastination in paying debts by a wealthy man is injustice. So if debt is transferred from your debtor to a trustworthy rich man he should agree"[170]*

---

[168] *ibid* p 167

[169] *idem* with editing for clarity

[170] Muslim, Ibn al Hajjaj al-Nis⁻aburi aka Sahih Muslim (died 261(AH)/875(CE)), quoted in Ayub p 168

Security for Loans (Kafalah)

One a loan is made the lender can ask for some security that will allow him to recover his debt if the borrower is unable to meet his commitments. This idea is in Sura 2:282 of the Quran:

"If ye are on a journey and cannot find a scribe a pledge with possession may serve the purpose"

Kafalah in Islamic commercial law effectively means guarantee. There are two forms of guarantee:

- Kafalah - guarantor
- Rihn - pledge/surety

Kafalah means to take on the responsibility for the payment of a debt or for a person's appearance in court. Legally...a third party becomes surety for the payment of a debt unpaid by the person originally liable. The degree or scope of [the guarantee] should be known and should not come with preconditions. It is a guarantee given to a creditor that the debtor will pay the debt, fine or any other liability.

Rihn, or pledge, is also a security for the recovery of debt if the debtor fails to repay it. Kafalah and Rihn...have different functions. In the contract of Kafalah, a third party becomes surety for the payment of debt, but in Rihn, the debtor hands over something as a pledge to ensure the payment of debt.[171]

Contracts for Kafalah or Rihn have to be based on mutual consent for them to be valid.

In the modern commercial context, Islamic banks can call for the following guarantees to secure loans that it makes:

- letters of guarantee
- promissory notes
- freezing cash deposits
- third party guarantees
- Hamish Jiddiyah - earnest money taken from a prospective client to ensure the performance of any assignment or liability by him before execution of the formal contract
- 'Arbun - downpayment taken as part of the settled payment taken after execution of the formal contract

Sale of Debt and Debt Instruments (Bai' al Dayn)

The sale of debt in secondary markets is a fundamental part of the Western model of finance. The rates obtained in these markets being an indication of the potential cost of issuing further debt. These markets are the subject of deep analysis without which many governments and institutional lenders

---

[171] *ibid* p 169 edited for clarity

would not be able to price their products are estimate the risk of entering a given market at given time. The figures quoted earlier for the pricing of US Treasuries are all based on mathematical models (the US Treasury says it's a cubic spline model) that are followed in near real-time in the money markets. It is almost impossible to imagine how the current world economic model could function without the secondary debt market.

The sale of debt at a discount – the basis of the secondary markets- albeit with some disagreement from some Malaysian jurists is prohibited:

> *The trading of Islamic bonds at a discount using Bai' al Dayn has been found unacceptable by the Jumhur Ulama' including al-Shafi'e. As such, the position of Malaysian Islamic bonds remains unacceptable among the Middle Eastern jurists, although some Malaysian jurists found this the opposite." The OIC Islamic Fiqh Council, which has the representation of all Islamic countries, including Malaysia, has also approved the prohibition of Bai' al Dayn unanimously...[172]*

Indexation against Inflation is Prohibited

One of the most called for 'rights' in the Western economic system is the cost of living increase. It is expected that, as the cost of a fixed basket of goods and services increases (or, conversely, depending on your perspective, the value of money decreases) there will be a compensatory rise in average salaries and wages and, on the other side, tax and related allowances.

This idea is completely forbidden under an Islamic financial system is it is nothing less than Riba. Ayub quotes Pakistan's most judge, Justice Khalilur Rahman, on the issue:

> ***Riba/interest cannot be rationalized on the basis of indexation*** *because all loans and debts are to be settled on an equal basis in terms of the units of loan or object. In the case of paper currency, exchange takes place by counting. If the debt contract amounted to Rs[173] 1000/- the creditor may claim only Rs 1000/- by counting – no more, no less. The prohibition of Riba essentially requires that, generally speaking, all like-for-like exchange be executed on an equal basis in terms of the relevant units of exchange.[174]*

The prohibition on Riba is pervasive in Islamic Finance. There has been much study since Islam began aimed at ensuring that Riba, in all its forms, is excluded from lending or borrowing. Indexation, whereby the value of someone's salary or purchasing power increases based only on time, is, quite simply, a Riba-based solution and is, consequently, forbidden.

---

[172] *ibid* p 172
[173] The currency abbreviated here is the Pakistani Rupee
[174] Shariat Appellate Branch (Pakistan), Justice Khalilur Rahman as quoted in Ayub *op cit* p 173

When someone lends money or goods it is a generous act, freely made. Compensation is prohibited. If the monetary or market value of the item returned is reduced (due to inflation, for example) then the act of lending is even more generous and has greater virtue before God.

Banks as Financial Intermediaries

Borrowing and Lending

Banks in the Western model act mainly as financial intermediaries. With a few exceptions, notably in Germany, they make profits based on the movement of money from one place to another and back again. Excluding those banks that act as money market connectors between treasuries and other banks for example, this money derives from deposits taken by banks/mutual societies from individuals with little, if any, significant purchasing power. These deposits are pooled together, with a small amount retained to meet normal withdrawal requirements[175], and then loaned out to those, such as small businesses, who need to borrow money for capital or other projects. The depositors are paid a small (currently less than zero in real terms) amount of interest, the lenders are charged a higher rate of interest and the financial organisation effectively uses the spread (that is, the difference between the two rates) to pay its bills and make a profit.

Banks have to carry out risk management to reduce the risk that the borrowers fail repay the principal and the interest. Indeed, the root cause of the current financial crisis lies in the manifest failure of financial organizations to take the time to understand the inherent risk in certain financial 'products'. However, after a loan has been made a bank will not be involved in the business at all and will now act only to get its money back. This suits both the bank and the business owner. The business owner gets the money needed to invest in his/her business for new equipment, training or premises, for example, and the bank, without getting involved in the day-to-day running of the business, gets a return for itself and (less so) for its depositors. The business owner, however, even if the business is not doing well, will be responsible for ensuring that the loan repayments are made in good time or risk being marked with a poor credit rating.

The Quran, Marx and Risk-Averse Lending

The idea that, even if the business fails, the bank should in any way be accountable and risk losing capital without a severe punishment, including potential bankruptcy, for the borrower is an almost alien concept in the Western model. The win-win nature of this system for the banks lies at the base of increasing disquiet and dissatisfaction among the public with how banks 'behave'. This is the capital, and its associated behaviour, that Marx discussed in his famous book on Capital.[176]. It is also the behaviour that the Quran (written down 1200 years before Marx) speaks against. The prohibition on Riba is to ensure that:

---

[175] This is the capital reserve ratio that has become the centre of much attention as some banks have over-leveraged themselves leaving little in reserve against unexpected changes in market conditions. It is hoped that, following such initiatives as the Basle III rules, the likelihood of a bank failing and losing its depositors money will be reduced.

[176] Marx, Karl Capital (1867). There are many translations from German, with commentary, available

> "(wealth) does not make a circuit between the wealthy among
> you" (Quran 59:7)[177]

On the other hand, the advantage of this system is that it is easy to
understand, simple to manage and above all quick and cost-effective to
implement.   Even if many people are not clear about how interest is
calculated their involvement with the bank reduces to the payment of an
agreed, simple to understand number each month. Like it or not, this is the
limit of most people's desire to engage with the management of their wealth.
It has been since goldsmiths started to manage gold deposits on behalf of
their clients.

So in the West we have a system in which money is loaned out at interest to
allow capital (money) to be placed where it is wanted. The system means
that banks in the 'western' system do not get involved to any great extent in
how a business runs after a loan has been granted because the loan contract
means all the money has to be paid back with interest against the possibility
of gaining a poor credit rating and facing bankruptcy; neither of which makes
getting credit in the future an easy task.   Working one's way out of
bankruptcy is a slow and difficult project. The system appears to encourage a
'dog in the manger' approach to business failure – whatever the reason for
that failure – if we can't get our money back (with interest AND penalties for
default) then we'll make sure you can't easily set up in business again.

How Do Islamic Banks Make a Profit?

As business lenders tend to require more money than most individuals hold
in their bank accounts, there will always be a need for financial
intermediaries. This leads us the question that if Islamic banks are prohibited
from charging or giving interest, how do they make a profit? How do they
attract investors to place money with them and then how do they charge the
borrowers so that they can create enough margin to pay their costs and even
derive a profit?

Islamic scholars and jurists recognise the need for banks and other financial
intermediaries in a modern and effective economic system: The words of
Jarhi and Munuwar make this clear:

> *Financial intermediation enhances the efficiency of the*
> *saving/investment process by eliminating the mismatches*
> *inherent in the requirements and availability of financial*
> *resources of savers and entrepreneurs in an economy.*
> *Entrepreneurs may require funds for periods relatively longer*
> *than would suit individual savers. Intermediaries resolve this*
> *mismatch of maturity and liquidity preferences by pooling*
> *small funds. Moreover, the risk preferences of savers and*
> *entrepreneurs are also different. It is often considered that*
> *small savers are risk averse and prefer safer placements*

---

[177] Quran sura 59:7 quoted in Ayub *op cit* p 129

whereas entrepreneurs deploy funds in risky projects. The role of the intermediary again becomes crucial.[178]

It should be clear then that banks are required but that their modes of operation under the Islamic Economic system must be significantly different to those in the western system.

The Basic Modes of Islamic Banking

The simple declaration that an Islamic bank cannot charge interest means that these institutions have had to develop, alongside Islamic scholars, jurists and economists, a range of financial instruments and techniques that do not occur (at least not to any significant extent) in the western system. According to Ayub:

> *The striking difference is that risks in Islamic banking remain with the ownership, as a result of which, IFIs share profit or loss arising on investments and earn return on their trading and leasing activities by dint of the risk and liability taken and adding value in real business activities. They mobilize deposits on the basis of profit/loss sharing and to some extent on the basis of Wakalah[179] against pre-agreed service charges or agency fees.[180]*

Islamic banking breaks down into two main approaches. Once again, Jathi and Munuwar give an excellent résumé of the ideas:

> *"As a rule, all financial arrangements that the parties agree to use are lawful, as long as they do not violate Islamic principles. Islam does not stop at prohibiting interest. It provides several interest-free modes of finance that can be used for different purposes. These modes can be placed into two categories. The first category includes modes of advancing funds on a profit-and-loss sharing basis. Examples of the first category are Mudarabah and Diminishing Musharakah with clients and participation in the equity capital of companies. The second category includes modes that finance the purchase/hire of goods (including assets) and services on a fixed-return basis. Examples of this type are Murabahah, Istisna'a, Salam and leasing".[181]*

The overall impact of this is that the basic mode of operation for an Islamic bank is trading. In western (conventional) banks, funds are provided for trading businesses but the banks do not get involved in the trading process.

---

[178] Munawar, Iqbal (2001) "Islamic and Conventional Banking in the Nineties: A Comparative Study", Islamic Economic Studies, 8(2), 1–27. Quoted in Ayub *op cit* p 186

[179] Wakalah is the Arabic term for agency. An agent is a person (physical or legal) who acts on behalf of second person with the full authority of the second.

[180] Ayub *op cit* p 186

[181] Jarhi and Munawar (2001) quoted in Ayub *op cit* p 187

In order to make a profit, an Islamic bank will have to undertake business with all its associated risks.

For example, rather than lend money to a business, with the associated impossibility of making any profit, an Islamic bank will purchase goods from a manufacturer using the money that it has available from its depositors. It will then add an agreed amount of mark-up to the cost of the goods and sell these on to the business that required them. In this way the bank becomes the owner of the goods and has to accept the full risks associated with ownership, that is, the right to sell them on but also the possibility that the business that ordered the goods decides not to buy them from the bank in the end. The business not taking the goods would be bad form (breaking a promise) but, nevertheless, the bank would have to take accept that and find a buyer elsewhere. For this reason the bank's risk management strategy has to be comprehensive. This type of credit sale is called Bai' Mu'ajjal and the two most important forms are:

- Musawamah – a normal sale, in which parties bargain on price, a sale is contracted and the goods are delivered while payment is deferred.
- Murabahah – a cost-plus sale, in which the parties bargain on the margin of profit over the KNOWN cost price. The seller HAS to reveal the cost incurred by him for the acquisition of the goods and provide all cost-related information to the buyer.

These modes of Islamic Finance are 'preferred' by experts in Islamic economics and are described in more detail in later chapters.

Islamic Banking Products Compared to Conventional Products

Islamic banks are working to provide the full range of services currently provided by western (conventional) banks. The following table gives a summary of the modes of Islamic finance used to cover different conventional products and services offered. The list is not exhaustive and some of the services will be more familiar in Islamic countries or in areas where agriculture, for example, is more common. Depositors will declare a preference for how their money can be invested or managed, if at all, when opening a particular type of account.

Conventional Product/Service	Islamic Mode
1. Use of Deposited Funds	
Current Deposit	Amanah – Loan (Qard) to bank. No return is payable
Savings Deposit	Mudarabah
Ordinary investment deposits	Mudarabah
Individual portfolios	Mudarabah

Conventional Product/Service	Islamic Mode
Liquidity creation	Tawarruq – reverse Murabahah, sale to a third party
2. Trade and Corporate Finance	
Project Financing	Musharakah, syndication through Mudarabah, Murabahah, Istisna'a, Ijarah/Ujrah
Working capital Finance	Murabahah, Salam and Musharakah
Export Finance – pre shipment	Salam/Istisna'a with Murabahah and Wakalah, Murabahah, Musharakah
Export Finance – post shipment	Qardal Hasan in local currency (spot rate) and promise to sell foreign exchange in future market – exchange rate differential is the bank's income. Murabahah if funds are needed for the next consignment
Import Finance	Murabahah, Musharakah
Cash Finance	Salam, Istisna'a and/or Tawarruq (sale to third party)
Letter of Credit	Commission, Ujrah along with Murabahah and others
Letter of Guarantee	Kafalah, service charges
3. Agriculture, forestry and fisheries	
Production finance for feed stock	Murabahah and Salam
Farm equipment (eg tractors)	Ijarah Munahia-bi-Tamleek, Salam and Murabahah
Livestock (such as cattle and sheep)	Murabahah and Salam
Storage and farm construction	Diminishing Musharakah or rent-sharing
Land development	Operating Ijarah and Salam
4. Treasury	
Money market – inter-bank	Mudarabah with or without allocation of assets
Liquidity management	Sale/purchase of permissible securities, parallel Salam, Tawarruq
Fund management	Mudarabah, Wakalatul Istismar and trading in permissible stocks and sukuk
Trading in sukuk and stocks	Depends on the nature of the traded instrument
Forex operations	Unilateral promise to buy/sell foreign exchange simultaneously at pre-agreed rate
5. Personal advances (consumer durables and housing)	
Consumer durables	Murabahah sale by instalments
Cars	Ijarah Munahia-bi-Tamleek, Murabahah
Housing finance	Diminishing Musharakah and Murabahah

Conventional Product/Service	Islamic Mode
Cash for personal needs	Salam if possible or Tawarruq

Preferred Modes in Islamic Banking

The majority of Islamic scholars prefer that the interest-based system should be replaced in an Islamic system by a profit and loss sharing (PLS), that is, a partnership-based system that encompasses Musharakah, Mudarabah and the slight variations on this theme. Although these PLS modes are less common at the moment, they are regarded as the norm that Islamic banking should approach as it matures. According to Umer Chapra:

> ...the most important and unanimously agreed upon form of financing provided by Islamic banks would be on the basis of Mudarabah, Shirkah or acquisition of shares of joint stock companies.[182]

Although the opinions are not unanimous, Chapra goes on to defend his position with the following rationale:

> The general principle, [as in any business], is that the financier cannot avert the taking of at least some risk if he wishes to derive an income. To put this in the form of an adage, one could state with respect to all financing operations: no risk, no gain[183]

This gives some Islamic scholars cause for concern as the aim is to avoid Gharar (uncertainty). However, as Chapra says, it is almost impossible to avoid all uncertainty as it is often in the uncertainty that possibility for trade and profit exists. The aim must be to reduce Gharar to an acceptable level through careful risk management and to ensure that any uncertainty is not uncertainty created deliberately with the intention that one party to a transaction gains an advantage over the other.

The Islamic scholars are not, however, Islamic bankers. It should be clear that PLS modes are time-consuming and management-intensive[184], so the issue becomes one of how to run a bank efficiently and effectively for profit while maintaining the required levels of socio-economic justice required by Islam.

Islamic bankers live in the real world of business where debt-creating modes[185] are common. These modes have been used throughout Islam's rich trading history as they are not prohibited by the Quran (The Prophet himself used them in his business transactions) and become, as a result, a matter of preference.

---

[182] Chapra quoted in Ayub *op cit* p 196

[183] *idem* [my clarification due to length of subordinate clause!]

[184] Khan and Mirakhor (1987) pp 125-161

[185] Debt-creating modes are created when someone (physical or legal) becomes obliged to pay something to someone else

Consequently, PLS and debt-creating modes together form the basis of the majority of Islamic banking modes although there is a scholarly preference for PLS modes.

There is a vast literature now in which the different modes and their costs and benefits have been analysed in computer-based simulations by various economists. Ayub summarizes some of the conclusions drawn from this modelling:

- Expectation-based profit-sharing ratios can serve as a pricing mechanism to bring the loanable funds market into equilibrium
- The elimination of risk-free assets with positive returns will leave lenders worse off
- Profit-sharing ratios are relatively inefficient instruments of monetary policy
- The introduction of interest-free banking does not necessarily lead to a situation where all profitable projects will be financed irrespective of their rate of return

One of the most interesting, perhaps obvious, conclusions is that where there is some risk the returns are generally higher. Ayub notes that:

> *Shirkah-based (PLS) modes that provide the much-needed risk-based funds can be used for short-, medium- and long-term project financing...This could generate higher rates of return for the investors relative to the return realizable on any interest-based investment.* [186]

Later chapters provide examples of how Islamic banking can operate at the level of small depositors.

The rest of this section looks briefly at how Islamic banks have approached (and with considerable success) the more difficult issue of investment banking. This is an area where there is more uncertainty (Gharar). The constant push for greater and greater profits combined with the repeal of laws promulgated specifically to protect small investors[187] following previous financial crashes has created a dangerous mix. If we then add to this the clear inability[188] of the regulators to comprehend and act against the selling of these new 'products' then we can see one of the main contributing factors to the current financial crisis. The uncertainty remains with major players in the global financial industry STILL unaware of how some 'bad purchases' made before the crisis will unwind. This has forced governments to 'bail out' the banks using tax payers' money and has resulted in the creation of 'bad banks'

---

[186] Ayub *op cit* p 198

[187] Glass-Steagall was repealed during Bill Clinton 's second term

[188] The regulators task has not been made easy. Some financial institutions have made it a matter of pride find ways around regulation and to make every effort to hide what they are doing behind layers of misdirection and even false declarations of suitability. Unfortunately, a large number of these institutions have been 'hoisted on their own petard' bringing down the global financial system as a by-product of their hubris.

the sole purposes of which is to hold toxic debt until it turns good – assuming it doesn't bring down the bad bank also. The Belgian state finds itself in a similar situation with the collapsed Dexia bank[189]. Some calculations estimate that the Belgian taxpayers ('les contribuables') will be at risk for another 70 years.

Islamic Investment Banking Introduced

Ayub clearly describes the main functions undertaken by Islamic investment banks writing that they:

> ...provide venture capital financing to small, medium and big companies in a number of sectors. They avoid involvement in prohibited and unlawful activities and offer services to all projects except those manufacturing or dealing with forbidden products and services, such as alcohol, pork, entertainment, interest-based financial services and the like. Their services relate to venture capital and corporate finance, including syndication finance, project finance and transactions in the capital markets. Asset management or management of funds includes equity funds, real estate funds as well as alternative investments in Ijarah and other. They engage in treasury operations for managing the asset–liability mismatch created by different tenors[190] of investment opportunities and different return profiles[191]

Most of the major instruments used in the Islamic financial markets are equity-based and many appear in the form of certificates called Sukuk (plural of Sak)[192]. That is, they are based on ownership (in this case, syndicated ownership in the form of a partnership) or the right to usufruct. Most of these equities are shares in appropriate (ie Shari'ah-compliant) companies but there are other instruments that represent ownership of assets for example:

- profit/loss sharing (Mudarabah/Musharakah), for example, instruments issued by Mudarabah and asset management companies
- rent-sharing in the form of Diminishing Musharakah or otherwise

A pure debt market is, of course, not a viable one under Islamic banking. This derives from the Quranic injunction that debt has to be repaid at the original value and one has to repay only the person who loaned the money out; unless a contract for Hawalah (assignment of debt) has been struck. When taking on a debt liability under Shari'ah, one has to have recourse to the original debtor under the rules of Hawalah. This is absolutely not the

---

[189] Dexia has been renamed Belfius

[190] Tenor in this context refers to the length of time that an investment is made (1 year, 5 years etc)

[191] Ayub *op cit* p 199

[192] Sukuk will be discussed in detail in a separate chapter.

case in the conventional system where paper debt is constantly changing hands from one holder to another in, for example, the secondary bonds market. The prices at which a nominal debt changes hands is used as an indication of how much a state will have to pay for its future debt. The volatility of these prices (measured using a statistic called duration) suggests how much the price of paper debt will change as interest rates change and the maturity date for the debt approaches. In effect, there is a constant game of 'musical debt' occurring as no one wants to be left holding debt that they've, perhaps, paid too much for.

Participatory Modes – Profit and Loss Sharing

The preferred mode in Islamic Finance is for profit and loss sharing. This is called participatory mode. The Islamic term for this mode is Shirkah. Shirkah-based participatory modes of business involve direct participation in profits and losses for the parties. The Shirkah mode falls into two types of contract called Mudarabah and Musharakah. Musharakah contracts, in turn, can be straightforward or a Diminishing Musharakah. The Diminishing Musharakah contract is a recent development of Islamic jurisprudence whereas the other forms have, in an almost unchanged form, been used since the early days of Islam.

Definition of Shirkah

> *Shirkah can be defined as a business where two or more people combine their capital or labour or creditworthiness together, having similar rights and liabilities, to share the profits or a yield or appreciation in value and to share the loss, if any, according to their proportionate ownership*[193]

The form of the Shirkah partnership will depend on the objectives and form of the partnership.

Partnership by Contract (Shirkatul'aqd)

The main form of Shirkah is called Shirkatul'aqd and is created by offer and acceptance between potential partners. The Accounting and Auditing Organization for Islamic Financial Institutions (AAOIFI) as 'an agreement between two or more persons to combine their assets, labour or liabilities for the purposes of making a profit'[194]

This type of partnership is created by a contract and partners are agents of one another. That is, any one member of the partnership can make binding decisions for the partnership. A partner cannot sell his/her share without the others partners' consent. This type of contract takes two main forms[195]:

Shirkah al 'Inan or General Partnership

Shirkah al 'Inan, involving collective capital of the partners, is where any two persons become partners in any particular business or where they become partners in all matters of commerce indifferently. It is contracted by each party…becoming the agent of the other and not his [guarantor]. This form enjoys consensus among all Islamic jurists. It is the most important form and seems to be nearer to the modern concept of a business partnership.

---

[193] Ayub *op cit* p 308
[194] AAOIFI, 2004, Standard on Shirkah (Musharakah) clause 2/1 p 200
[195] Ayub *op cit* p 310 [I have made some edits for clarity]

Shirkatula'mal

Shirkatula'mal, or Sanai' [is] a partnership in labour or crafts... where two persons become partners by agreeing to work jointly, and to share their earnings, in partnership. This type of includes, for example, partnerships between doctors and lawyers.

Mudarabah

Mudarabah is a partnership in the profits of capital and labour. One partner provides the capital (Maal) and the other party provides labour.

Structure of a Business under Shirkah al 'Inan

Shirkah al 'Inan is a flexible type of contract that can be adapted to a range of business situations and fits in well with modern business practices. According to Ayub:

> *It refers to a joint enterprise formed for conducting any business with the condition that all partners shall share the profit according to a specified ratio, while the loss will be shared according to the ratio of contribution to the capital of the joint business. Two or more partners that are considered agents (Wakil) of [the] other partners share the business on the basis of the following conditions:*
>
> *1. Capital can be invested by the partners in any proportion.*
>
> *2. Power of appropriation in the property and participation in the affairs of the Shirkah may be different and disproportionate to the capital invested by the partners.*
>
> *3. Profit may be divisible unequally and disproportionate to the capital invested, and may be according to the agreement of the partners.*
>
> *4. Loss is to be shared in proportion to the capital invested.*
>
> *5. Each partner is an agent to the other partners.*
>
> *6. No partner is responsible for indemnification of the acts of commission and omissions on the part of other partners.*

There are differing opinions on the rights of partners to do certain things with the business but these, being in the realm of Islamic jurisprudence, are beyond the scope of an introductory text.

Basic Rules for a Musharakah Contract

As with all contracts, Musharakah must be agreed with the free consent of all parties involved, there must be no deception, misrepresentation, duress and Gharar must be reduced to the greatest extent possible concomitant with running a modern business. There are Musharakah specific conditions that also need to be fulfilled.

Those entering a contract must be free individuals (imprisonment is considered a temporary inhibition), have legal majority and be of sound mind. A minor can enter into a Musharakah with the permission of a guardian. It is possible for a contract with a non-Muslim to be agreed and also to carry out business with interest-based banks if certain conditions are carefully adhered to. Ayub observes that:

> ...*arrangement has to be made to obtain all necessary assurances and guarantees that the rules and principles of Shari'ah will be observed during the operation of the partnership. It excludes all those businesses which are not lawful in Islam, i.e. trade in swine flesh or liquor, etc and unlawful activities like pornography and gambling. For example, if a syndicate of banks comprising Islamic as well as conventional banks is financing any huge project or corporate firm, the Islamic bank's portfolio must comprise valid contracts like Ijarah to ensure its Shari'ah compliance. In this respect, a distinction has to be made between the goods and activities which are absolutely prohibited for all and the goods and activities which are prohibited for Muslims alone. Interest, for example, is prohibited for all in an Islamic state, while alcoholic drinks and flesh of the swine, etc are prohibited for Muslims alone. A non-Muslim citizen of an Islamic state can be permitted to trade in the objects of the latter category but partnerships in any such trade will be declared void if any of the parties is a Muslim[196]*

This would appear to imply that all the partners in a Musharakah partnership that traded in, for example, pork or alcohol would have to be non-Muslim.

Capital Brought in to a Musharakah Contract

The majority opinion of the jurists is that capital invested by a partner should be in liquid assets whose value is known without ambiguity. Whether these assets are in the form of currency or goods is left to local practice with the condition that the value of the goods must be translated into a known currency value at the start of the contract. Debt cannot be used as a start-up capital until it has been received. This suggests that the partners can agree to someone joining on the basis of debt due to be paid before the business commences trading.

Relationship among Partners and Management of Musharakah

A Shirkah-based business is managed according to the will and equal right of all the partners acting as agents for one another. Any ownership of assets brought into the business becomes collective, that is, owned items are in the constructive possession of all the partners.

---

[196] *ibid* p 313

In addition:

> ..all partners in a Shirkah have a right to take part in management of the joint business in the following transactions: cash or credit sales, rejecting defective goods, renting the partnership's commercial assets, cancellation of contracts, requesting credit facilities for the partnership, taking the partnership's receivables, making payments or giving deposits and providing or receiving pledges for the partnership and doing all that is customary in the interests of the joint business.[197]

However, Ayub goes on to point out that:

> Working for the joint business by each partner is not necessary and it can be agreed in the partnership agreement that the management will be restricted to a single or some identified partners, in which case the other partners should not act on behalf of the partnership. The partners can also agree to appoint a manager other than from the partners and pay him a fixed remuneration that will be treated as an expense of the Shirkah[198]

If there are no conditions to the contrary, then partners may also exercise the following rights under Musharakah:[199]

- To invest the Shirkah capital in Mudarabah
- To make any person an agent for any work in the Musharakah
- To keep the property of Musharakah with any person as Amanah or deposit or give it as a loan
- To mortgage the property of Shirkah
- To travel for the concerned business at the expense of Shirkah
- To become a partner in any other Musharakah on behalf of his own Shirkah business
- To mix the property of Musharakah with that of his own
- To accept the mortgage of property of any outsider on behalf of his Musharakah
- Depending upon consent of the other partners and the 'Urf, spending any sum out of the Musharakah property
- To purchase and sell goods necessary for the conduct of business

Treatment of Profit and Loss

The distribution of profit and loss is one of the most important aspects of business partnership under Shari'ah. As partners have the right to put in

---

[197] *ibid* p 315
[198] *idem*
[199] *idem*

different amounts of capital (although there contracts where this is not permissible)[200] they are entitled to an appropriate share of the profits. However, the share of the loss is strictly in line with the ratio of capital invested. Generally, the share of profits is in line with the share of capital brought in but this does not have to be the case.

To avoid any ambiguity, the generally accepted view is that:

> ...the ratio of distribution of profit must be agreed upon at the time of execution of the agreement, otherwise the contract will not be valid in Shari'ah.[201]

A very important consideration is that the monetary value of the profit must not refer back to the monetary value of the capital invested. **Only the profit represents the true value of a business**. If a partner's return was based on the monetary value of the capital invested (not its ratio in the overall capital of the business) this would amount to nothing more than Riba.

However, any loss incurred by the business must be borne in exact ratio to the money invested. This principle can be traced back to the fourth Caliph of Islam, Ali who is credited with the following maxim:

> "Profit is based on agreement of the parties, but loss is always subject to the ratio of investment"[202]

There is complete unanimity among the jurists on this point. The AAOIFI standards do, however, allow one partner to bear voluntarily the entire loss at the time of the loss. This cannot be made a precondition of the partnership.

Taking a Lump Sum out of the Business

Partners are entitled to draw lump sums out of the business subject to the condition that the investment ratios will be adjusted if the amount drawn exceeds the profit entitlement at the end of an accounting period. This is because the partner will reduce his invested capital if the profit is too low or a loss has been made. Partners are also allowed to renegotiate the terms of their contract.[203]

Guarantee in Shirkah Contracts

The assets in a Shirkah partnership are in the form of a trust. This means that no one individual is liable for losses except in the cases of breach of contract, misconduct or proven negligence. Ayub lists the cases where negligence can be deemed to have occurred[204]:

- a partner does not abide by the terms and conditions of the contract

---

[200] For example, Shirka al Mufawadah is a contract in which everything is shared on an equal basis.
[201] ibid p 316
[202] AAOIFI, 2004, Standard on Musharakah, p. 221 quoted in Ayub op cit p 317
[203] AAOIFI, 2004, Standard on Musharakah clause 3/1/1/4 and 3/1/5
[204] Ayub op cit p 318

- a partner works against the norms of the concerned business
- the established ill-intention of a partner

This means that the profit or even capital of any partners cannot be guaranteed by the co-partners. However, one partner can demand from another partner to provide any surety, security or pledge to cover the cases of misconduct and negligence.

Maturity and Termination of Partnership

A Musharakah contract is non-binding. This means that any partner can withdraw his share from the partnership at any moment he chooses. However, it is permitted that the partners agree on a timeframe for the life of the partnership. Traditional Shirkah agreements terminate in the following circumstances[205]:

- When the purpose of forming Shirkah is achieved in the case of a specific purpose Musharakah. While the profit will be distributed according to the agreed profit distribution ratio, any loss will be borne by each partner according to the ratio of his investment
- When, after sufficient information or notice, any partner withdraws from a partnership after giving his partners due notice to this effect. His withdrawal will not necessitate termination of the partnership between the remaining partners. Assets will be distributed pro rata among the partners with mutual consent and then the profit, if any, will be distributed on the basis of the agreed ratio. It is preferable that assets are assessed in terms of monetary value with mutual consent
- When any partner dies. However, his heirs can replace him with the consent of the other parties
- When the whole of the Musharakah capital is exhausted or lost
- When any partner is prevented or prohibited from exercising his legal powers over his property

Shirkah partnerships were originally conceived during a time and in a place where caravan trading was the prevalent mode for a trading business. This type of partnership had a short definite duration so early termination was not really a consideration. However, in the complex nature of modern businesses some jurists have contended that any partnership with more than two partners remains extant after the withdrawal of a partner. It is, however, permitted that partners can sell their share in a partnership to someone else. This is similar to the way limited companies, especially companies listed on a public exchange, manage changes of ownership.

---

[205] *idem*

Mudarabah

Mudarabah[206] is a type of Shirkah partnership where an investor or a group of investors (there is no limit on numbers) (rabb-ul-maal) provide capital to an agent or manager (*mudarib*) who has the responsibility to invest it in a commercial enterprise. The profit in the business is shared in line with a pre-agreed ratio between the investor(s) and the manager/agent. Any capital loss must be borne solely by the investors. The agent will lose for the time and effort that has been put into the business for which there will not be remuneration. The social importance of this type of contract was recognised at the time of the Prophet. The 11th century Hanafi scholar, Al-Sarakhsi, notes that:

> ...people have a need for this contract. For the owner of capital may not find his way to profitable trading activity and the person who can find his way to such activity may not have the capital. And profit cannot be attained except by means of both of these, that is, capital and trading activity. By permitting this contract, the goal of both parties is attained[207]

Mudarabah fulfils an important economic function that encourages the hiring of capital and trade skills on the sensible basis of risk-taking. It is hoped that this has benefits both for society and the concerned parties.

Mudarabah contracts require trade in lawful items otherwise the contracts become void or, at least, voidable. The majority of contemporary jurists see the use of Mudarabah being widespread in a range of businesses as an alternative to interest-based financing. Mudarabah contracts are based on trust and the Mudarib:

> ...is considered trustworthy with respect to the capital entrusted to him. He is not liable for the loss incurred in the normal course of business activities. As a corollary, he is liable for the property in his care as a result of the breach of trust, misconduct and negligence. A guarantee to return funds can be taken from him but can be enforced only in two situations: if he is negligent in the use of funds or if he breaches the stipulated conditions of Mudarabah. Hence, his actions should be in consonance with the overall purpose of the contract and within the recognized and customary commercial practice. In some situations, he becomes an employee when he performs some duty after the Mudarabah contract becomes invalid.

Mudarabah Capital

The capital invested in the partnership should be in the form of a currency. This is to avoid any ambiguity as to the value of any capital invested. This is

---

[206] The term is synonymous with Qirad and Muqaradah. Mudarabah was common practice at the origin of Islam and Islamic teachings have confirmed its legality

[207] Al-Sarakhsi quoted most likely from his *Mabsut* in Ayub *op cit* p 322

especially true of illiquid assets. The use of debt is, as always, not permitted – the capital must be free from all liabilities in order for it to be invested. All the capital is put into a single pool and appropriate profit ratios are agreed at the beginning of the contract. No one is permitted to assign a particular portion of a profit to a particular portion of capital or to say that the profit from this particular transaction belongs to one partner or another (assuming that more than one investor is involved).

Combining Capital

It is possible by the writing of careful contracts for a Mudarib to invest in the Mudarabah contract in which he is involved. In this case, there will be a mixture of Mudarabah and Musharakah contract - the Mudarib will be become a partner in a Musharakah contract to the extent of his portion of the investment and a worker/agent in the Mudarabah contract for his remaining contribution. As an example, if we imagine a bank acting as Mudarib for a group of bank depositors. The rabb-ul-maal (depositors) and the bank (mudarib) agree that they will share the profit 50:50. Normally, the bank does not invest and its return will be limited to 50% of the profit of the Mudarabah contract with the bank in the role of Mudarib. However, the bank may decide to add further funds to the contract resulting in the creation of a Musharakah contract.

If the depositors put in €2000 and the bank €1000, for a total of €3000 invested, then the bank's share (Musharakah) is 1/3 of the profit (whatever figure that is). If the profit on the contract is €300 then the bank will get €100 as Musharakah profit and will get a further €100 as 50% of the remaining €200 profit. The depositors will get €100. This will be allocated to the depositors in a ratio that matches each depositor's individual contribution. It should be clear from this simple example that Islamic banking certainly requires a tight control over its administrative procedures.

Restricted and Unrestricted Mudarabah

The freedom of the Mudarib to invest may be limited by the investor(s). Ayub quotes the following from the AAOIFI standards:

> *Mudarabah business can be of two types: restricted and unrestricted Mudarabah. If the finance provider specifies any particular business, the Mudarib shall undertake business in that particular business only for items and conditions and the time set by the rabb-ul-mal. This is restricted Mudarabah. But if the rabb-ul-mal has left it open for the Mudarib to undertake any business he wishes, the Mudarib shall be authorized to invest the funds in any business he deems fit. This is called unrestricted Mudarabah. In both cases, the actions of the Mudarib should be in accordance with the business customs relating to the Mudarabah operations: the subject matter of the contract.*[208]

---

[208] AAOIFI (2004) quoted in Ayub *op cit* p 324

The rabb-ul-mal has the right to impose conditions as long as they do not prejudice the interests of the business and the purpose of Mudarabah. These conditions may include (the list is not exhaustive) that the rabb-ul-maal[209]:

- may fix a time limit for the operation of the contract
- may specify the articles to be traded in or whose trade is to be avoided
- may stop the worker from dealing with a particular person or a company
- may stop the worker from travelling to a particular place or may also specify the place where trade is to be carried out
- may ask the worker to make sure to fulfil his fiduciary responsibilities (but not profitability)
- may (according to some jurists) compel his worker to sell the goods if the bargain is profitable (while the worker wants to hold then)
- has a right to stop the worker from contracting a Mudarabah with any other party

The mudarib is bound to follow the rabb-ul-maal's conditions. If he violates a restriction or contravenes a condition he…

> …becomes a usurper and will be responsible in respect of capital to the capital owner. He is not entitled to sell the Mudarabah goods at less than the general market price or buy goods for Mudarabah at a price higher than the common market price. He is also not allowed to donate Mudarabah funds or waive receivables of the business without explicit permission from the financier[210]

In the traditional formulation the rabb-ul-maal is not permitted to work for the business. The aim in the past was to give the worker discretion over his work but also to meet the purpose of the contract, that is, bring together capital and expertise. This idea is slowly changing with the times and the current advice is that parties may agree any role for the investor at the start of the contract. However, the rabb-ul-maal always retains the right to oversee that the mudarib is doing his fiduciary duties honestly and efficiently.

Sharing of Profit and Loss under Mudarabah

The two parties are free to make an agreement stating the proportion of the profits that each one is entitled to. This agreement must be made at the time that the contract is agreed. No fixed sum arrangement is permitted. However, the entire loss is borne solely by the financier unless it can be shown that the mudarib has been deliberately negligent in exercising his duties.

The profit-sharing ratio can be changed with the agreement of all partners.

---

[209] Ayub *op cit* p 324
[210] *idem*

The Timing of Profit-Taking

Profits are calculated over an agreed period of time. At the end of the agreed period the accounts will be closed off and the profit that is to be shared is calculated, taking into account the retention of profits for the protection of capital. To ensure that there is no cause for dispute, all expenses to be paid and any receivables need to be quoted in their cash equivalent before calculating the final profit figure.

Termination of the Mudarabah Contract

A mudarabah contract is non-binding. This means that any of the parties to the contract can terminate it unilaterally. The contract cannot be unilaterally terminated:

- when the Mudarib has already commenced the business, in which case the contract becomes binding up to the date of actual or constructive liquidation
- when the parties agree on a certain duration of the contract, in which case it cannot be terminated before expiry of that period except with mutual agreement[211]

In preparing to terminate the contract, the Mudarib must be given time to sell any illiquid assets so that cash value for the profit can be calculated.

Although, the right to terminate unilaterally is a part of the Mudarabah contract, it does not violate any principle of Shari'ah if the partners add a condition to the contract saying that none of the partners can terminate the partnership until an agreed period of time has elapsed.

Brief Comparison between Musharakah and Mudarabah

The table below summarizes the main differences;

---

[211] AAOIFI (2004) quoted in Ayub *op cit* p 327

Subject	Musharakah	Mudarabah
Investment Source	All partners provide capital	Investment from a person or a group of people (Rabb-ul-maal) but not the contractor (mudarib)
Right to Participate	All partners have the right to participate	Rabb-ul-Maal has no right to participate in management, but can participate if desired, especially to ensure the mudarib meets his fiduciary duties
Loss Attribution	All partners share the loss of capital according to the ratio of their investment. The loss is unlimited and can exceed the initial investment if bad decisions have been made.	Only the Rabb-ul-Maal is liable for losses unless the mudarib has been demonstrably negligent and therefore liable to incur debts appropriately.

Modern Corporations under Islamic Finance

Modern corporations are, in effect, based on the ideas of Shirkah al 'Inan as a combination between Musharakah and Mudarabah contracts. The most common way in which these ideas are used in in the form of a joint stock company in which a large number of people provide funds and receive, in return, receipts called shares or similar certificates. These shares certificates represent the proportionate ownership of the business. Ayub quotes the AAOIFI standard on Musharakah which describes a stock company as:

> ...an entity, the capital of which is distributed into equal units of tradable shares with limited liability of the shareholders to their pro rata capital. The rules relating to Shirkah al 'Inan are applicable to it except on the issue of the limited liability of the shareholders. In other words, shareholders are owners of the assets of the company to the extent of shares held by them. They can sell/transfer the shares to any other persons but have no discretion over the assets of the company[212]

The last sentence in the definition is important. The owners are not involved in the day-to-day running of the company and have no powers to wind the company up. Those powers are delegated through a company's Articles of Association to the Board of Directors, who are in turn responsible for assigning people to run the company day-to-day. This is the same separation that occurs in western company law. The Musharakah 'right to participate' comes through regular shareholder meetings, through which the owners can impose conditions on the members of the Board.

Preference Shares are not Shari'ah-Compliant

Preference shares are shares that allow their holders preferential treatment. Usually this consists of access to profits before other shareholders. Under Shari'ah, no gain can be had unless there is an undertaking to bear the risk of

---

[212] Ayub *op cit* pp 328-329

loss. This means that all shareholders must be treated alike, based solely on the number of shares held by each of them. If shares are issued that gives preferential treatment, for example, shares that protect the shareholder from any losses incurred then this is Riba because it guarantees a return based on investment not on profit.

Share Trading after a Float May Amount to Riba

The purpose of floating a company is to raise cash for the purchase of assets for the company. As these shares initially represent money only (no physical assets have been purchased) and not any underlying assets they can only be traded at the price paid for them (the face value of the certificate). To trade them otherwise is Riba. One of the parties will make money with money if the shares are sold at a different price. However, as soon as the liquid assets have been used to buy tangible assets then the price paid for these shares is a matter between seller and buyer as long as the price is a fair reflection of market value. It is not required that the shares represent ONLY tangible assets. Some liquid cash and, certainly, intangible assets such as the patents, copyrights and similar can be counted but the proportion of the shares representing these assets needs to be appropriate.

There is no complete consensus among the jurists of the different schools on the ratio. The Hanafi jurists take the view that:

> ...a combination of liquid and tangible assets can be sold/purchased for an amount that is greater than the amount of liquid assets in the combined assets. They prescribe no specific proportion of tangible assets to qualify for permission of such a sale/purchase. However, most of the contemporary scholars, including those of the Shafi'e school, have allowed trading in the shares and certificates only if the non-liquid assets of the business are more than 50%, while some reduce this floor to 33%[213]

This, clearly, implies that running a joint stock business like this under Shari'ah is a challenging administrative task.

Diminishing Musharakah

As the name suggests, a Diminishing Musharakah (DM) contract is a contract whereby a party to the contract promises to reduce his share by promising to sell a portion of his share to the other partner or partners. This share is usually sold in agreed amounts and the seller's participation in the contract diminishes over time. All the jurists are clear that this is a permissible type of contract under Shari'ah.

There are two types of DM contracts; contract by ownership (Shirkatulmilk) and partnership by contract (Shirkatul'aqd)[214].

---

[213] *ibid* p 130
[214] See the chapter on contracts

In Shirkatul'aqd (the most common type), the ratio of profit distribution is a matter for the parties to the contract. The amount of loss taken by each partner depends on the ratio of the partnership held at the time the loss is declared. However, the price paid for shares in the business cannot be decided in advance. The contractual nature of the business means that no one individual owns any particular piece of the business (see Musha'a below) and the partners are not permitted, therefore, to decide in advance the price of any share.

In Shirkatulmilk, the price of the shares sold at each point can be agreed in advance (because the items are **owned**). This is vital in the Islamic Finance version of a mortgage, which will be discussed later.

The DM contract is also dependent on the legal enforceability of a promise, which the jurists agree means that a court of law (under Shari'ah) can compel a promisor to fulfil his promise. This is especially true in the context of commercial activities.

Overcoming the Issue of Undivided Ownership (Musha'a)

DM contracts also need a solution to the issue of Musha'a or undivided ownership. Within a Musharakah contract a partner cannot specify what assets or parts of assets belong specifically to him. Everything belongs to everybody. How then can one decide which parts are to be sold back as the involvement of the partner decreases?

The answer, which has unanimous support of the jurists, takes the following form:
- partners agree to enter into a Musharakah contract
- the 'leaving' partner agrees to lease his **share** to the other partner or partners
- the 'leaving' partner sells his **share** to the other partner or partners

This requires three separate contracts, none of which can be dependent on the others. The three contracts are:

Partnership (Musharakah) – this brings in money from a financier to allow a business to commence trading through the purchase of stock and other assets

Leasing (Ijarah) – this allows the financing partner to gain profit from the usufruct of his share in the company's assets. This proportion will be reducing over time as his share decreases.

Sale (Bai') – the partner regains his investment in portions on the sale of his share. His profit comes from his share in the usufruct which is diminishing.

Use of Diminishing Musharakah in Islamic Financing

The commonest uses for DM in the modern Islamic Financial system are to allow businesses to operate leasing contracts for fixed assets (eg plant and machinery) and to allow people to buy cars and homes (mortgages).

Shari'ah scholars have agreed that three contracts are entered into separately. This ensures that each contract is independent of the other two contracts. The sequencing of contracts should be:

- A contract [is created] between partners to create a joint ownership. The client partner makes a promise, before or after the lease agreement is finalized, to purchase the share of the financier partner
- The financing partner gives units of his share to the client on lease
- The client partner goes on purchasing the units of ownership of the financing partner as per his promise. Accordingly, the rent goes on decreasing[215]

Requirement to Acquire DM Shares is Not Binding

If it seems a good idea on the part of the a businessman to keep on buying shares in his business on a DM basis, Shari'ah scholar s have agreed (through the OIC Fiqh Academy) that such purchases cannot be made binding on him. The requirement to offer these shares for sale to the businessman is, however, binding on the financier in the contract. Ayub summarizes this as follows:

> ...after creating joint ownership, the bank may sign a one-sided promise to sell different units of the share of its ownership periodically and may undertake that when the client purchases a unit of its share, the rent of the remaining units will be reduced accordingly. Thus, an Islamic bank will be making a binding promise to offer a specific part of its ownership of the project for sale on a specified future date for a price that will be determined at the time of actual sale. The entrepreneur partner may voluntarily buy the share of the financier at the prices prevailing at the time of sale in the stock market or at a price determined with the free consent of the parties[216]

Case Study – Mortgage using DM

The process is best understood through a common example; the purchase of a house. Most people cannot afford the purchase price of a house so they need to access finance usually from a bank or mutual society. If we imagine a house that costs €240.000 and that the bank is willing to meet €200.000 of this cost with the remainder being paid by the purchaser. It is proposed that this contract will last for 10 years (120 months) and that the bank cannot charge any interest for the money that has been borrowed. How does the bank make a profit if it doesn't charge for the money? The answer is a DM arrangement is created whereby the bank becomes joint owner in the Musha'a of the property. The buyers will pay an agreed monthly rent through an Ijarah-based leasing agreement to the bank which is the co-owner

---

[215] Ayub *op cit* p 339
[216] *ibid* p 340

of the property. The rent will decrease over time as the buyers buy an increasing share of the property from the bank. After an agreed number of payments the buyers become sole owners of the property.

The monthly payments consist of two components, one is for the purchase of units of ownership from the bank and the second is the rent payable to the bank for the share of the property that the bank owns.

If we imagine that the bank and buyers agree that a fair rent for the bank's (diminishing) share of the property would be 2.5%, then we can create a schedule of payments to the bank that clearly shows the progress of the mortgage.

A Rental Charge is Not Riba

The bank's 2.5% charge is not interest; it is an agreed price for the use of the bank's property. The buyers are not paying for money – they are paying for the use of property each month. The payment is the bank's entitlement to usufruct for property that it owns. The rent payable is not related to the amount of capital borrowed rather it is related to an agreed value for the use of the property.

Rental Rates can be Fixed or Floating

The agreed rental can be fixed at the beginning of the contract or it can be allowed to float (variable). To avoid any suggestions of Gharar, the variable rental will have to be subject to a cap and floor agreed within which the rent can move. This will ensure that the mortgage transaction is Shari'ah-compliant.

Month	Unit Price (P/Units) €	Rental €	Total €	Units Remaining	Principal (P) Remaining €
1	1.666,67	416,67	2.083,33	120	198.333,33
2	1.666,67	413,19	2.079,86	118	196.666,67
3	1.666,67	409,72	2.076,39	117	195.000,00
4	1.666,67	406,25	2.072,92	116	193.333,33
5	1.666,67	402,78	2.069,44	115	191.666,67
...	...	...	...	...	...
119	1.666,67	6,94	1.673,61	1	1.666,67
120	1.666,67	3,47	1.670,14	0	-

Table 1 Schedule of Payments for DM Mortgage

Commercial Contracts

Shari'ah prohibits banks making a profit from the lending of money. This means that they are required to engage in trading, which is, in fact, their most common activity. Rather than lend money, banks can make a profit by being part of the trading process. This is done through several different contract types and the use of, for example, securitization in the form of Sukuk.

Ayub summarizes this idea as follows:

> *[an] Islamic bank's trading pattern is different from the general trading business. [The] bank's clients normally need a credit facility [so] the banks [sell] goods on credit... creating receivables. Credit sale (Bai' Mu'ajjal) may take a number of forms, important among which are:*
>
> *1. Musawamah, or normal sale, in which parties bargain on price, a sale is executed and goods delivered while payment is deferred*
>
> *2. Murabahah, a "cost-plus sale", in which parties bargain on the margin of profit over the **known cost price**. The seller has to reveal the cost-incurred by him for acquisition of the goods and provide all cost-related information to the buyer[217]*

Murabahah is used extensively by Islamic banks where it is deemed crucial even if it is discouraged by Islamic economics and finance experts in favour of Profit and Loss modes.

Murabahah

A Murabahah transaction is:

> *...concluded with a [] promise to buy or a request made by a person interested in acquiring goods on credit from any financial institution. As such, it is called "Murabahah to Purchase Orderer" (MPO). The AAOIFI's Shari'ah Standard on Murabahah is also based on this arrangement.[218]*

For a Shari'ah-compliant Murabahah, there are many issues to take into account. For of all, the sale must be valid under Shari'ah and meet, for example, all of the conditions of a Valid Bai' including, but not limited to, free and mutual consent of the parties to the transaction, certainty of price, certainty of date and place of delivery and certainty about time and payment of the price. The seller must be the owner of the items for sale and they must be in his physical or constructive possession and the item must be transferable, allowing the buyer to assume the risks of ownership.

---

[217] *ibid* p 213 (I have made some edits for clarity)
[218] *idem*

Murabahah is a Fiduciary Sale

The starting price in Bai' Murabahah is the original cost or purchase price. This form requires an honest declaration of the cost by the seller. The buyer and the seller start from this point until they reach agreement about the profit margin for the seller. This can be compared to Musawamah in which the buyer has no reference to the original cost of the item and where the final price is fixed in terms of value for the two parties.

> By definition...for a valid Murabahah...the buyer must know the original price, additional expenses if any and the amount of profit. Accordingly, Murabahah is a contract of trustworthiness[219]

Murabahah is for Restricted Situations

The main feature of a murabahah sale is its requirement for complete honesty and openness on the part of the seller. It is fiduciary in nature, based on a level of trust between the buyer and the seller. It is therefore open to abuse. Consequently, jurists prefer the straightforward musawamah contract where buyer and seller negotiate openly without the need for information to be declared. Ayub quotes Imam Ahmad:

> To me, ordinary sale (Musawamah) is easier than Murabahah, because Murabahah implies a trust (reposed in the seller) and seeking of ease on behalf of the buyer, and it also requires detailed description to the buyer; there is every likelihood that selfishness may overcome the seller, persuading him to give a false statement or that mistake may occur which makes it exploitation and fraud. Avoidance of such a situation is, therefore, much better and preferable[220]

However, modern Murabahah is, in the main, carried out by Islamic banks on a deferred payment basis. However, the issue of trust is not a serious one as the customer is involved to a great extent in the locating and purchasing of the goods.

Specific Conditions for Correct Murabahah

- Goods to be traded should be real but not necessarily tangible
- Money **cannot** be traded (murabahah is a credit transaction)
- Documents representing debt **cannot** be traded
- The seller must state the original price and any costs added to bring it to market
- All aspects of the item must be declared by the seller
- Margin of profit has to be by mutual agreement

---

[219] *ibid* p 216
[220] *idem*

- The units used to describe the price must be known
- Incorrect statements will render the contract void
- Buyer has option to return if, after purchase, undeclared defects are found. This is true even without a specific option clause

Clearly, murabahah is a lawful sale that can be used as a useful alternative to interest-based transactions. At the same time it is clear that it has significant limitations and even when used by banks there are many issues that need to be thought about carefully to ensure Shari'ah compliance.

Expertise Needed for Murabahah Trading

On the issue of murabahah trading Ayub is clear. It is complex:

> *Trading and other real sector business activities require specific expertise, which bankers may or may not have. Further, it is not possible for banks to train all staff in trading, marketing and other real sector activities required for Islamic banking practices. One possible solution is that banks may establish specific purpose companies to undertake trading (and leasing) activities and the staff with relevant specialized expertise may be entrusted the job of trading in goods so as to fulfil the Shari'ah essentials of Murabahah–Mu'ajjal[221]*

The bank may opt to use any of the following techniques:
- Trading carried out by the management of the bank. This would be good from the point of view fulfilling murabahah essentials but would be a difficult managerial task.
- Use of a third-party or an agent; This would be a good option as it would mean good management and Shari'ah compliance especially around the issue of taking possession of goods before they are sold on to the clients.
- Use the client as an agent. Research has shown that this opens the door to the hiding of interest-based transactions.

For a detailed overview of these issues please consult Ayub's book.

Forward Sales: Bai Salam and Istisna'a

There is a futures market within the Shari'ah framework. At first this idea seems to break all the rules for what is considered to be a valid sale. Remember that the three conditions are that:
- the commodity to be sold must exist
- the seller should be the owner of the commodity to be sold
- the commodity must be in the physical or constructive possession of the seller

---

[221] *ibid* p 220

Salam and Istisna'a are exempt from the above on the grounds that some conditions have been met through the establishment of trust and the provision of adequate detail about the deliverables. It is important to note that this type of futures market is not the type dealing in options, derivatives and swaps.

Bai Salam is an ancient type of forward contract in which advance payment was made for **prescribed** goods to be delivered later.

> Salam has been permitted by the holy Prophet (pbuh) himself, without any difference of opinion among the early or the contemporary jurists, notwithstanding the general principle of the Shari'ah that the sale of a commodity which is not in the possession of the seller is not permitted[222]

The seller undertakes to supply specific goods to the buyer at a future date in exchange for an advance payment made in full at the time of contract. The quality of the commodity to be purchased must be fully specified leaving no ambiguity that could lead to dispute.

Ayub quotes a hadith of Imam Bukhari:

> Upon migration from Makkah, the Prophet came to Madinah, where the people used to pay in advance the price of fruit (or dates) to be delivered within one, two and three years. But such a sale was carried out without specifying the quality, measure or weight of the commodity or the time of delivery. The holy Prophet ordained: "Whoever pays money in advance (for fruit) (to be delivered later) should pay it for a known quality, specified measure and weight (of dates or fruit) of course along with the price and time of delivery[223]

Benefits of Bai' Salam and its Economic Role

The Bai' Salam contract has been allowed under Shari'ah with a structure that renders it free from Riba, Gharar and the possibility of the exploitation of one party by the other. Under Shari'ah the contract is:

> ...based on genuine need of the business and, therefore, beneficial to both buyer and seller. The seller gets in advance the money he needs in exchange [for the] obligation to deliver the commodity later. Thus, he benefits from the Salam sale by covering his cash/liquidity needs in respect of personal expenses or for productive or trading activity. The purchaser gets the commodity he has planned to trade at the time he decides. He will also benefit from cheap prices, because usually the Salam price is cheaper than the cash market price. This way he will also be secured against fluctuations of price[224]

---

[222] *ibid* p 242

[223] This hadith is quoted in the AAOIFI standard (2004) p 171

[224] Ayub *op cit* p 242

Features and Conditions of Valid Salam Contracts

The subject of a Bai' Salam contract is an important feature. The consensus is that anything that can be precisely described in terms of its quality and quantity can be the subject of a Salam sale. The subject must be fungible which means that the subject is not defined to be one particular item (a particular tin can from a particular factory, to give a silly but germane example). The contract, rather, should give a description of the quality of tin cans required for delivery as well as the quantity. A Salam contract cannot be made where the subject for sale and the consideration are the same. In the modern Salam contract the jurists agree that:

> All goods that can be standardized into identical units can become the subject of Salam...The subject should generally available in the market[225]

Salam Cannot be used for Currency Trade

Currencies must be exchanged only hand-to-hand. There can be no delay as this would amount to Riba (any delay would give one person twice the wealth while disadvantaging the other). As a Salam contract involves deferred payment currencies cannot be the subject of a Salam contract.[226]

Salam Capital

It is perfectly acceptable to pay Salam capital in terms of goods as well as legal tender. The usufruct of assets can also be assigned at the time of the contract. Although this appears to break the rules on debt (as something of immediate value has not been exchanged, there must be a debt), there is a:

> ...legal maxim that says: "Taking possession of a part of a thing is like taking possession of the whole thing". Hence, making usufruct capital of Salam does not mean debt against debt, which is prohibited.[227]

However,

> Outstanding loans/debts due [by] the seller cannot be fully or partially fixed as price, nor can a loan outstanding on a third party be transferred to the seller in future adjustment towards the price, as this amounts to an exchange of obligation for obligation(debt for debt), which is forbidden.[228]

Place and Time of Delivery

A Salam contract requires the precise definition of the place and time of delivery. Historically, Salam contracts allowed delivery often up to three

---

[225] *ibid* p 244

[226] There is a minority dissenting juristic opinion on this issue that has led some Islamic banks to trade Salam with currencies.

[227] *ibid* p 247

[228] *idem*

years after the contract was struck. The modern scholars recommend that a place and date be known (as close as possible in the case of the products of a harvest of wheat for example). Delivery can be made in instalments but the subject will remain at the risk of the seller until delivery. If no place of delivery is in the contract then the place where the contract is struck is deemed to be the place of delivery. Options are not permitted in a Salam contract.[229]

Revocation and Penalty for Default

The Salam contract can only be revoked by mutual consent. In this case, the buyer is entitled to his money back (no more and no less – which would amount to Riba). However, the may be situations where the seller cannot deliver. There may no longer be the particular subject matter in the market at the time of delivery. In this case, the buyer may decide to accept other goods in the place of the contract's subject matter.

If the seller fails to deliver for any reason except an absence of the subject matter in the market he should pay a penalty, although the inclusion of a clause in the contract to that effect is not permitted.[230] In the event that a penalty is payable to a bank or other financial institution, then this money will have to be added to a Charity account as the bank cannot charge what would, in effect, be interest on the value of the undelivered items.

Reselling goods Purchased on Salam

Under the normal rules of sale, the buyer cannot sell the goods on until he has taken possession of the goods. This is because the rights of ownership remain with the seller until delivery. The problem is that without the ability to do this in a Salam contract it would be next to impossible to create an Islamic banking system. Most jurists have, therefore, permitted the onward selling of goods in a Salam contract as it is not specifically prohibited in the Quran, Sunnah, Ijma'a or Qiyas.

Parallel Salam – *sine qua non* for an Islamic Banking Future

Parallel Salam is the selling on of goods purchased in a Salam contract before they have been delivered. Part of the rationale for the acceptance of this is that the price risk is transferred to the purchaser as soon as the contract has been made. There is no way to know which way the price will move between contract strike and delivery. This risk is considered an acceptable reason to call Parallel Salam a legitimate trade under Shari'ah. Not all jurists accept the logic of this argument. However, in the bigger picture of a push for what is believed to be a more equitable financial system, this may be a small compromise to make.

---

[229] *op cit* p 248
[230] Clause 5/7 of AAOIFI Salam Standard

Istisna'a

Istisna'a is the manufacturing equivalent of a Salam contract. Someone wishing to buy a particular manufactured item pays up front while specifying the nature and quantity of the required items. They are delivered as soon as possible after manufacture, or on the delivery date agreed in the Istisna'a contract.

Ijarah - Leasing

Ijarah derives from an Arabic expression, al'Ajr, which can be translated as compensation, consideration, return or counter value. As an idea under Islamic Finance, it refers to:

> ...hiring or renting any asset/commodity to benefit from its usufruct. It also encompasses the hiring of labour and any contract of work for anyone against a return (wage). Therefore, broadly the rules and principles of labour, renting, Ju'alah and all other contracts for usufruct of goods and services are covered by the term Ijarah[231]

As a legal contract, Ijarah refers to the:

> ...transfer of usufruct for a consideration, which is rent in the case of hiring assets or things and wages in the case of hiring people. According to the jurists, Ijarah is the sale of usufruct (not...goods) of any commodity in exchange of Ujrah, wages or rent, and covers houses, shops, riding/work animals, jewellery, clothes, etc.

The essential features of Ijarah, therefore, are that:
- It is a legal contract
- It requires the transfer of a known usufruct
- A known asset is involved
- A known time period is agreed
- A rental is agreed

Ijarah is therefore analogous to leasing in the conventional business sense. In an Ijarah contract, like a Bai' contract, something is transferred to another person for a known consideration and the full details of the contract (what is exchanged for what) must be clear before the contract is signed.

Vital Difference Between Bai' and Ijarah

In Bai' the ownership of something (tangible or otherwise) with all its associated risks is transferred from one person to another. In Ijarah, the ownership of something is not transferred; only the right to make use of and make monetary gain (if that is the aim) of whatever usufruct has been transferred. The Ijarah contract details the cost and other conditions of that

---

[231] Ayub op cit p 279

temporary ownership of use. If for any reason the lessee comes to own the object of the Ijarah contract, the contract ceases to be valid.

Valid Subject Matter for Ijarah Contracts

Not everything can be the subject matter of an Ijarah contract. Ayub describes the essential features as follows:

> *Ijarah is valid for things which possess Manafa'ah and which can be hired or utilized but their corpus or substance ('Ayn) is not consumed. Goods like candles, cotton, food or fuel are suitable for sale, not for leasing or hiring.*

Clearly then, edibles, fuel and raw materials cannot be leased as they are consumed during their use and money cannot be leased as it would be no more than an exchange of money for money. The lease would be invalid. Further, if it's not possible to make use of the leased subject matter then the subject matter cannot form part of an Ijarah contract. For example, land hit by salinity to the extent that it is not capable of any producing crops cannot be leased out.

Conditions for a Valid Ijarah Contract

Ayub quotes Al-Kasani who sets out some basic conditions for the execution of an Ijarah contract. These are set out below[232]:

- The exact nature of the contracted usufruct must be known to avoid any dispute
- The lease period must be specified. However, in the case of a wage/service, either of the two, ie the nature of the work or the time required for a job should be known
- It must be possible to benefit from the hired goods. It is not permitted to contract a lease if the usufruct cannot be determined precisely
- The rent is not due until the subject of the lease is delivered and made available to the lessee. The mere execution of the contract is not enough although advance rent can be taken when availability of the usufruct is ensured
- The contractor should be capable of undertaking the job. So, for example, hiring a plumber to carry out electrical work is invalid
- The purpose of the Ijarah contract should not be unlawful. The usufruct of the contracted subject must be Halal
- The usufruct should be conventional or according to the tradition of the people

---

[232] The list is paraphrased from Ayub *op cit* pp 281-282. I have paraphrased because Ayub translated the passage from Urdu which makes heavy use of passive sentences

Setting and Adjusting the Rent in Ijarah

The two parties agree on the rent to be charged for the contract. When the contract is struck, the lessor cannot unilaterally increase the rent without voiding the contract. In long-term leases, however, it may be necessary to write an appropriate clause into the Ijarah contract allowing the rent to increase. The use of a well-defined reference rate or benchmark is recommended to avoid any dispute or injustice caused by market fluctuations beyond the control of the contracting parties. The use of an RPI figure is permitted as it is a figure that is external to the Ijarah contract. However:

> *...the Shari'ah scholars do not like any interest-related benchmark for determining periodical increases in the rental due to the resemblance to interest. In principle, however, they allow it because the basic difference between valid lease and interest-based financing is that in leasing, the lessor assumes full risk in respect of the corpus of the leased assets. If the leased asset loses its usufruct without any misuse or negligence on the part of the lessee, the lessor cannot claim the rent and he will have to bear the loss of destruction. In the case of interest-based lease financing, however, the lessee is made to bear all ownership-related expenses and responsibility. So far as this basic difference (of assuming the risk) between lease and interest-based financing is maintained, any transaction will not be categorized as an interest-bearing transaction.[233]*

It is, however, desirable to use benchmarks other than interest benchmarks to ensure that there is no resemblance between un-Islamic and Islamic transactions.

Sub-lease under Ijarah

Sub-leasing is permitted if permission is included in the Ijarah contract. The sub-rental charge is a matter for agreement between the original lessee and his sub-lessee. However, the contract for the sub-lessee must ensure that the right to benefit from the usufruct has been transferred. No lessor has the right to take rent unless appropriate ownership risks have been transferred. The rent from an Ijarah contract cannot be shared (as a business proposition) unless ownership risk has been shared among all those sharing in the rent. Each partner collecting rent must have ownership risk ie he must accept the risk of loss of the asset, damage to the asset or, for example, a change in the viability of land that has been leased.

The lessor can demand an appropriate guarantee from the lessee. The lessee can only be held responsible for damage to property rented to him if wilful negligence can be demonstrated.

Termination of Ijarah

An Ijarah contract is binding. The contract remains in force until:

---

[233] Ayub *op cit* p 284

- its agreed termination date
- the usufruct is no longer available
- the two parties agree that it should end

Any other type of termination is "contrary to the principles of justice and equity and, therefore, un-Islamic"[234]. In the event that the usufruct is no longer available, research should be carried out with the aim of remediation. Repairs might be made or, in the case of a reduction in available usufruct, a reduction in rental might be a more just and equitable solution.

The death of lessor or lessee is not a reason for the automatic termination of an Ijarah agreement. The lessee's heirs may, however, decide to terminate if the "contract has become too onerous for their resources to pay the rental"[235]. All advances of rent will have to be repaid in the event of early termination of the contract.

Default on the Ijarah Rent

Ayub summarizes the issue of non-payment of rent, which is in effect a debt, and as such non-payment of debt:

> ...will be subject to all rules prescribed for a debt. Therefore, a charge from the lessee on the agreed rental would be Riba, prohibited by the Shari'ah. Unscrupulous lessees could exploit this aspect and cause loss to the lessor by wilful default. To provide a deterrent, Shari'ah scholars allow that a donation or any amount of penalty payable to charity can be provided **ab initio** in the lease agreement; the amount of donation can vary according to the period of default and can be calculated on a percentage per annum basis. Any amount charged over and above the agreed rental must not become a part of the income of the lessor and has to be given to charity. As this late payment penalty cannot become part of the income of lessor banks, it is advisable that a suitable clause be incorporated in the lease agreement to the effect that in cases of wilful default, the bank will take possession of the leased asset or enforce the collateral to recover its dues

Modern Use of Ijarah

Leasing is a major part of the modern financial services world. It ranges from airlines leasing planes from the manufacturers to train companies leasing rolling stock from specialist leasing companies such as Porterhouse. Many households use leasing under the common heading of hire-purchase for cars, fridges, washing machines, PCs etc. Ayub remarks that:

---

[234] *ibid* p 286
[235] idem

In Islamic finance also, leasing is an important instrument with a lot of potential in the business of Islamic financial institutions, not only because of these benefits but also because of the "Asset-based nature" of investments in Islamic finance. From the Islamic perspective, leasing operations by banks and financial institutions are governed by the rules prescribed in Fiqh for Ijarah transactions.[236]

Financial Lease (Hire-Purchase)

In the conventional system, it is hire-purchase that looks most like Ijarah but there are some differences. The most significant differences are that the client is responsible in the sense of ownership for the asset and its maintenance (although this varies with the company managing the lease) and the client is often required to start paying rent before delivery of the product. Most companies will allow the return of a malfunctioning product against a replacement, but some (as I'm sure some of us have experienced) make it harder than others. In the event of a default on payment there will be penalties to pay which amount to interest paid on interest (This is Riba and is forbidden under Shari'ah).

It is also usual that, at the end of the lease period, the lessee takes ownership of the asset following the payment of a small fee. All of this is included in the single contract signed at the beginning of the hire-purchase agreement. In effect the hire-purchase is made up of a rental contract and a sales contract all rolled into one with the sales contract effective only from a future date. This is distinctly un-Islamic. Consequently, Islamic jurists have had to work hard to create an equivalent form that meets the requirements of Shari'ah.

Combining Ijarah and Bai'

The Ijarah and Bai' contracts are different. Ijarah transfers the right to usufruct of something but not ownership; Bai' transfers all ownership rights and responsibilities. If someone in an Ijarah contract comes to own the leased object then the Ijarah contract is void. Ayub describes how the contemporary Islamic scholars have developed a lease agreement form that is Shari'ah-compliant.

Contemporary Shari'ah scholars recommend that a lease agreement should not contain a precondition of sale or gift after the lease period. However, the lessor may enter into a separate unilateral promise to sell the leased asset at termination of the lease. The principle, according to them, is that a unilateral promise to enter into a contract at a future date is allowed, whereby the promisor, say the bank, is bound to fulfil the promise, but the promisee is not bound to enter into an actual purchase contract. This means that the lessee would have an option to purchase, which he may or may not exercise.

---

[236] *ibid* p 287

However, if he wants to exercise his option to purchase, the promisor cannot refuse it because he is bound by his promise.

This *modus operandi* is called Ijarah Muntahia-Bi-Tamleek.

Ijarah Muntahia-Bi-Tamleek

Under Ijarah Muntahia-Bi-Tamleek, Islamic banks normally purchase an asset in response to a specific request from a customer. The asset is purchased on a lease using Ijarah and at the end of the lease period ownership is passed to the customer through one of the following means (this is based on the AAOIFI standard for Ijarah):

- By means of a promise to sell for a token or other consideration or by accelerating the payment of the remaining amount or by paying the market value of the leased property
- By promise to give it as a gift (for no consideration) at the end of the lease period
- By promise to gift contingent on a particular event, for example, upon the payment of the remaining instalments

Ayub provides an in-depth analysis with case studies of the issues surrounding Ijarah in his book, "Introduction to Islamic Finance"[237]

---

[237] Ayub (2004) *op cit*

PART FOUR – Other Aspects

Islamic Finance has sought to provide the same sort of financial services as the Western model. This is a complex process when the religious element has to be considered. Some might even argue that the whole process is costly as the number of layers of compliance is significant. Indeed, some of the 'products' are complex but the Islamic world has at least risen to the challenge of thinking differently about the problem.

Sukuk

In order to permit the funding of significant projects – those with costs in the multi-millions or even billions – there must be some sort of debt-creation. The money has to come from somewhere. Less than thirty years ago, under a Shari'ah-based system, it would have seemed that the only way large amounts of money could be raised for this type of project would be through equity-based solutions that allowed those with money to share in the profits of the project. However, many of these projects have long timescales and some, such as infrastructure projects (road, railways, schools etc), have little, if any, commercial return value. This makes it difficult to raise the required sums of money as the shareholders have to wait a long time before dividends are declared the money will go elsewhere.

The Bond Market

Under the conventional system, governments and large companies raise the required levels of cash by issuing bonds. The bonds give a regular interest-based pay-out (6-monthly or yearly, for example) meaning that investors don't have to wait an indeterminate period before getting some return on their investment. At the known maturity date the principal is repaid to the lender. However, under Shari'ah, debt cannot generate a return as it must always be sold on at face value with recourse to the original debtor through Hawallah. A conventional bond market could not exist if discounting (that is, the selling of a debt for less than its face value) were not permitted. The challenge, which has been met in full, for the contemporary jurists, was to create a Shari'ah-compliant market with the money-raising power of bonds.

Sukuk

Sukuk is the plural of Sak, the Arabic word for a financial certificate. Sukuk are the Shari'ah-compliant equivalent of securities such as bonds and allow some of the features and benefits of a debt market are possible even in an Islamic financial structure. The major requirement for Shari'ah compliance is that the certificate should not represent interest-bearing debt as the dominant part of the underlying assets. For example, the sukuk "issued on the basis of Shirkah and Ijarah represent the ownership of the underlying assets by the sukuk holders"[238]. This means that they can be traded (in the secondary sukuk market) at prices determined by market forces. This type of securitization process can, therefore, subject to certain conditions that ensure Shari'ah compliance, be used to create facsimiles of conventional bonds usable in an Islamic Finance system.

Ayub gives a clear résumé of sukuk as follows:

> ...Sukuk represent common undivided shares in the ownership of underlying assets with the effect that the Sukuk holders share the return as agreed at the time of issuance and bear the

---

[238] Ayub op cit p 390

loss, if any, in proportion to their share in investment. Issuance of Shari'ah-compliant Sukuk would result in enhanced supply of risk-based capital with limited risk-taking on account of the prohibition of Riba, gambling and Gharar and a balanced return rate structure based on real-asset-backed economic activities.[239]

Securitization and Sukuk

Securitization refers to a process in which the ownership of some underlying assets is transferred to a large number of investors in the form of financial instruments, which under Islamic Finance are referred to as sukuk. The securitization process is a complex mix of legal, technical, financial and other issues which need not be discussed in detail although under Shari'ah a lot more work has to be done to reduce the levels of Gharar to a minimum. Once again, Ayub presents a clear overview of the process:

> *The ownership of the securitized assets is transferred to a special purpose vehicle (SPV) or special purpose Mudarabah (SPM) that is set up for the dual purpose of managing the assets on behalf of the Sukuk holders and for the issuance of the investment certificates. The SPV that serves as Mudarib manages both the liabilities and assets of the issues. The contractual rights attached to Sukuk determine the mutual ownership and benefits of the securitized assets for the individual investors who subscribe to the Sukuk. The Sukuk holders earn any revenue generated by the project and/or capital appreciation of the assets involved.*[240]

As Islamic finance structures are by their nature asset-backed, this provides a large number of opportunities for the issue of sukuk for the funding of large projects which may be infrastructure-related and supported by a number of guarantees that may be State-backed.

Investment Sukuk Differ from Common Shares

Shares represent ownership of a company as a whole. They exist indefinitely, subject to decisions made by their boards, and there is no guarantee of any return on investment. A company's board retains the right to declare a dividend or not[241]. Sukuk represent specified assets and exist for a given amount of time (tenors extending more than 10 years are now available). Returns from sukuk are based directly on cash-flows from the securitized assets on which they are based.

Investment Sukuk Differ from Obligations (Bills, Notes and Bonds)

---

[239] *idem*

[240] Ayub *op cit* p 392

[241] This is despite the fact that, theoretically, it is the shareholders who choose the board, this is rarely, if ever, happens with Fortune 500 or similarly-quoted companies

The main differences between investment sukuk and obligations issued by central banks and similar organizations are described in the table below.[242] One of the most important differences is that sukuk investors must accept the potential for loss as well as profit. Holders of obligations such as bonds receive the coupon rate only; there is no underlying asset bar the trust residing in the issuing organisation or country.

Obligations (eg Bills, Notes and Bonds)	Sukuks
Obligations are not linked to shares	Each sukuk represents some part of the total shares underlying the financial operation
Obligations return a fixed revenue as interest on a regular basis	There is no interest paid to subscribers
There is no connection between the obligations and the financial results of the issuer	Subscribers are entitled to a part of the profit of the operation but they are equally liable for any losses
There is no connection between the due date of the obligation and any supported project (if such a specific item exists)	The term for any given *sukuk* is the length of the project being financed

Sukuk Investments Require Significant Management Effort

There are a number of parties involved in the creation of a sukuk. Some of the main participants are:

- The originator (the Sukuk issuer) sells its assets to an SPV and uses the realized funds for whatever project is in mind
- The SPV is an entity set up specifically for the securitization process and to manage the issue. The SPV purchases specified assets from the originator and funds the purchase price by issuing sukuk
- Investment banks act as underwriters and tale the lead in managing the actual issue. This is fee-based involvement only
- Sukuk subscribers are the people and legal entities who invest in the sukuk and would include, for example, central banks, Islamic banks, non-banking financial institutions (eg insurance companies and pension funds) and individuals

Different Types of Sukuk Allowed Under Shari'ah

In line with the AAOIFI sukuk may be constructed from different the contract types permissible under *Shari'ah*. This often leads to complex financial instruments that require careful construction and monitoring. For example, there are:

- Mudarabah sukuk
- Musharakah sukuk
- Ijarah sukuk
- Salam sukuk

---

[242] This is taken directly from Causse-Broquet *op cit* p 81 (my translation)

- Istisna'a sukuk
- Muzara'ah sukuk
- Musaqah sukuk
- Mugharasah sukuk

The sukuk considered to have the greatest potential are those based on Shirkah, Ijarah, Salam and Istisna'a (the first five in the list).

Mudarabah Sukuk

According to Ayub Mudarabah sukuk Mudarabah sukuk... Mudarabah sukuk...

> ...can be instrumental in enhancing public participation in investment activities in any economy. These are certificates that represent projects or activities managed on the Mudarabah principle by appointing any of the partners or any other person as Mudarib for management of the business. As regards the relationship between the parties to the issue, the issuer of Mudarabah certificates is the Mudarib, subscribers are the owners of the capital and the realized funds are the Mudarabah capital. The certificate holders own the assets of the Mudarabah and the agreed upon share of the profits belongs to the owners of capital and they bear the loss, if any.[243]

The most important features of these sukuk are detailed by resolution of the Islamic Fiqh Council.[244]

Musharakah Sukuk

In a Musharakah sukuk each subscriber is given a Musharakah certificate representing his proportionate ownership of the assets in the project. The intermediary party in a Musharakah sukuk will be one of the investors according to the rules of a Musharakah partnership. The certificates can be treated as negotiable instruments only after the project to which they relate has started. Profit is shared according to the agreed ratio set when the contract was agreed and loss is shared on a pro-rata basis.

This type of instrument has been used by the Sudanese government for long-term infrastructure projects.[245]

Ijarah Sukuk

Ijarah is basically a lease that permits someone to gain profit from usufruct. The usufruct derives from the leased property but the contractor doesn't (and must not in Ijarah) own the property that he is profiting from.

If the lessor (the owner of the physical asset that is leased) then:

> ...he can sell the leased asset wholly or partly, either to one party or to a number of individuals. The purchase of proportion of the asset can be evidenced by issuing certificates, which may be called Ijarah certificates or

---

[243] Ayub op cit p 398
[244] Resolution of the Fiqh Council of the OIC (fourth session, 1998)
[245] Ayub (2002) pp 128-131

Sukuk. The certificates must represent ownership of the pro rata undivided parts of the asset with all related rights and obligations. Hence, Ijarah Sukuk are the securities representing ownership of well-defined and known assets tied up to a lease contract, rental of which is the return payable to the Sukuk holders.[246]

The AAOIFI standard[247] allows Ijarah sukuk to be based on the following scenarios:

- Sukuk of ownership in leased assets
- Sukuk of ownership of usufructs of existing assets
- Certificates of ownership of usufructs to be made available in the future as per description
- Certificates of ownership of services of a specified supplier
- Certificates of ownership of services to be made available in the future as per description

The important part to note about all the above is the work done to avoid Gharar; suppliers must be specified, services must be as described.

Salam Sukuk

A Salam contract is created when a fixed price is paid for future delivery of the contract subject matter. The AAOIFI standard on Salam allows for the creation of a parallel Salam contract in which the Salam subject matter can be sold on. The requirement is that the two contracts are separate and can be enforced separately if required. The Salam seller (the issuer of the certificates) has to deliver the goods at the agreed date and time. The basis of the Salam sukuk is that cash can be raised against delivery of goods before the goods are delivered. The tenor for these contracts is short, usually in the region of 3-6 months and they are best based on Salam trade in heavily-traded (liquid) assets such as crude-oil, cotton or other products having a firm demand.

Secondary trading of Salam sukuk (that is, trading beyond the parallel Salam element) is considered unacceptable as it represents a share in Salam debt (which is money-based) for a contract which is based on units of the item for sale. This means, and the point is a subtle one, that a Salam contract that is sold on, being a debt, does not specify the units of the original subject matter. This is not permissible under Shari'ah.

Istisna'a Sukuk

Istisna'a is a contract for the manufacture of goods. It allows cash payment in advance and future delivery or future payment and future delivery. These sukuk can be used to finance the construction of houses, bridges and other infrastructure projects. Islamic banks and other financial institutions use a Parallel Istisna'a contract to ensure that ownership of the manufactured

---

[246] Ayub (2007) *op cit* pp 400-401
[247] AAOIFI, 2004-5a pp 298-302

(constructed) item is transferred from the contractor upon completion of the work. The deferred sales price covers all costs plus any profits accruing to the bank or institution paying for the project.

The manufacturer will issue Istisna'a sukuk to the people/organizations that are funding the completion of the goods or constructed building. They will own the item as it is constructed. When the project is completed the second parallel Salam contract ensures that the real purchaser of the item takes ownership at an agreed price (through a promise to purchase). The difference between the final price paid and the money raised in the sale of the sukuk represents the profit for the sukuk holders.

Istisna'a sukuk are only redeemable at maturity but they can be transferred at face value before that date. As always with Islamic financial products the purchasers of the sukuk run the risk of the certificates losing value if the market price for the produced items falls. This is unlikely in the case of long-term infrastructure products.

Issues with Sukuk' Shari'ah Compliance

An examination of Sukuk issues in different countries shows that a number of them are guaranteeing fixed returns. This is something that is completely forbidden under Shari'ah and a subject that has been research in great depth by Islamic scholars to establish the best way forward. In some cases the returns to investors are being boosted by using some of the issuer's profit to offset any loss – this may be an acceptable approach. However, it is less clear about what happens when losses are incurred (ie there are no profits to offset losses over the period of the investment?) As Ayub points out:

> The loss of the cost of funds that cannot be recovered under Islamic finance and expenses that could be incurred by the lessor as owner of the leased asset may not make it possible to give a return to Sukuk holders that is fixed and guaranteed in all respects[248]

Further:

> The Shari'ah scholars are unanimous that any pre-fixed return or guarantee of the investment by any of the partners in contractual Shirkah-based modes is not acceptable. According to the AAOIFI's Standard on Sukuk, a prospectus to issue any certificates (not only those which are Shirkah-based) must not contain any clause that the issuer is liable to compensate certificate holders up to the nominal value in situations other than torts and negligence, or that he guarantees a fixed percentage of profit.

However, it is possible for a third-party to provide:

- a guarantee, which must be free of charge and subject to conditions or,

---

[248] Ayub 2007 *op cit* p 409

- insurance

This leads us on to the subject of Islamic insurance.

Takaful (Islamic insurance)

Life and business are risky endeavours and throughout history groups and societies have taken measures to mitigate the impact of misfortune. Insurance against loss was recorded in the Code of Hammurabi in the second millennium BCE. If a loan was made to fund a shipment, repayments would be cancelled if the shipment was lost. There are references to insurance in the Talmud and the citizens of Rhodes developed a system whereby merchants who shipped their goods together paid into a pool from which losses were met if one of the ships was lost. Benevolent and Friendly societies have served the same purpose and still do today.

There was no real system of contractual insurance under Islam. There is also no direct reference to insurance in the Quran. However, members of Muslim societies are required to help each other, particularly in times of misfortune. Consequently, there have certainly been arrangements made to assist traders and other communities but nothing that might be easily compared to the modern insurance industry.

Is Taking Insurance to Question Allah's Actions?

The idea that taking insurance may question the will of Allah is considered by Ayub to be a myth. The purpose of Shari'ah is to save human lives from hardship. He quotes the Quran:

> **Allah wants for your ease, and he does not want to make things difficult for you (2:185)[249]**

He then relates a story of the Prophet:

> *One day the holy Prophet (pbuh) saw a person leaving a camel in the jungle, he asked him: "Why don't you tie down your camel?" The person answered: "I put my trust in Allah." The Prophet said: "Tie your camel first; then put your trust in Allah."[250]*

The Islamic scholars have taken it upon themselves to develop a scheme that enables human beings to avoid misfortune and to lessen the losses in a manner that complies with Shari'ah. Takaful was developed in response to the growth of Islamic Finance, the first example of which appeared in the late 1970s. Ayub believes its development was most probably a result of banks needing loss mitigation that was the driving force.

The Shari'ah scholars pronounced that conventional commercial insurance is unlawful under Shari'ah. This is due to the involvement of[251]:

- Riba (interest)
- Qimar
- Maisir (gambling)

---

[249] Holy Quran quoted in Ayub (2007) *op cit* p 418
[250] Ayub *op cit* p 418
[251] *op cit* p 419

- Gharar (unnecessary risk and uncertainty)
- Invalid transfer of risk from the insured to the insurer

Conventional insurance practices were clearly going to make it difficult to develop a Shari'ah-compliant alternative!

Riba in Conventional Insurance

The element of Riba is present in the act of using a small deposit (the policy premium) for a potential huge gain (the sum insured). Additionally, the insurance companies providing the cover are involved in Riba-based transactions in the financial activities in which they engage. It is possible to have paid monthly or yearly premiums for one's entire life and receive nothing tangible in return, that is the insurance company retains all the money.

Gharar, Qimar and Maisir in Conventional Insurance

There is often uncertainty (Gharar) about the subject matter of the contract (details of exclusions in insurance contracts can be difficult to work through). Receiving a payment from the insurance company isn't always a straightforward process even if the companies must protect themselves from potential fraud.

All insurance contracts fall under the heading Qimar where the gain of one side is entirely dependent on the loss of the other side. If there is no claim the insurance company "wins"; if there is a successful claim, the insurance company "loses". This is also designated Maisir in which monetary gains are derived from "mere chance, speculation and conjecture and from work, taking responsibility or real sector business"[252].

Ayub's description is a drastic oversimplification of the intellectual work that goes in to assessing the levels of premiums to be paid. This is done using vast amounts of data collected and detailed statistical analysis made by insurance companies in order to mitigate and hedge risks. Intellectual effort is praised under Islam and intellectual services can be bought and sold legitimately under Shari'ah. Why not the intellectual services behind conventional insurance? However, one must accept that premiums are set to maximize profit for shareholders in a competitive market that doesn't always have the policy holder's best interests at heart. A table comparing the two types is at the end of this chapter.

Where one party "gains" at the expense of another there is always going to be opportunistic behaviour; the chance for a quick profit to be made is almost irresistible. This is clearly recognised under Shari'ah or there would not be prohibitions originating in the Quran. If conventional insurance, whatever the intellectual warrant of the arguments against it are, is unacceptable under Shari'ah we must then ask, "What is the Shari'ah alternative?"

---

[252] *idem*

The Shari'ah Basis of Takaful

The provision insurance of under Shari'ah:

> ...requires that the nature of the main insurance contract should be converted to a contributory arrangement in which the losses to members may be covered from the Takaful pool on the basis of mutual help and sacrifice[253]

Under Shari'ah, therefore, a cooperative and social insurance scheme is legitimate as opposed to non-cooperative schemes with the qualities of gambling, temptation and usury that make the conventional insurance contract an invalid one. The principle of Takaful has its foundations in ancient Arab tribes and was approved by the Prophet. In the event of some disaster, all members of the tribe would contribute something until the problem was relieved.

> Islam accepted this principle of reciprocal compensation and joint responsibility. In addition, such an institution of mutual help was established in the early second century of the Islamic era when the Arabs expanding trade into Asia mutually agreed to contribute to a fund to help anyone in the group that incurred mishaps or robberies during the sea voyages.[254]

Elements of Takaful

Takaful insurance is based on shared responsibility, common benefit and mutual solidarity. "Every policyholder pays his subscription in order to assist those among them who need assistance"[255].

Tabarru'

The main part of the Takaful contract is a donation called Tabarru'. A party to a Takaful contract agrees to give up, as a donation, all or a part of his Takaful contributions, in order to fulfil his obligations of mutual help in the event that any of the other parties to the contract suffers a defined loss. The losses of the unfortunate few are shared by the contributions of the fortunate many. The members of the cooperative share the risk and the reward as the donated funds managed under the Takaful contract can be used in any Shari'ah-compliant way to generate profit for the members of the group as well as cover losses suffered by a party to the contract. The fund manager would be compensated through a fee for services or may share in the profit from the pool according to the details of the contract drawn up.

Sharing in Takaful is a Virtuous Act

Ayub makes it clear that providing a safeguard for your family through Takaful or an Islamic life policy is in line with the words of the Prophet:

---

[253] *ibid* p 420
[254] Ayub *op cit* p 421
[255] *idem*

> *"It is better for you to leave your offspring wealthy than to leave them poor, asking others for help". The holy Prophet (pbuh) also encouraged the providing of security for widows, orphans and the poor, as he highlighted in one of his sayings: "The one who looks after and works for a widow and for a poor person (dependent), is like a warrior fighting for the cause of Allah (SWT), or like a person who fasts during the day and prays throughout the night"[256]*

It is a perfectly legitimate act to run Takaful as a business. The only issue is to ensure that all business actions under Takaful are:

- Shari'ah-compliant
- transparent in their operation
- fair to all stakeholders

How a Takaful Company Operates

Ayub gives an excellent résumé of how a Takaful company operates in the business world:

> *A Takaful company serves as a trustee or a manager on the basis of Wakalah or Mudarabah to operate the business. The operator and the partners who take any policy contribute to the Takaful fund. Claims are paid from the Takaful fund and the underwriting surplus or deficit is shared by the participants. In life policies, a part of the contribution is also kept as an investment fund. The operator uses the funds in the business on the basis of Wakalah or Mudarabah. The underwriting surplus or deficit belongs to the policyholders/partners, while distribution of profit arising from the business depends upon the basis of Wakalah or Mudarabah.[257]*

If the Takaful company is working as mudarib the contribution paid by policyholders is divided into two parts:

- a protection part
- a savings and investment part

The protection part uses the tabarru' in the form of Waqf[258] and the investment and savings part is used to generate a profit for the policyholders or offset a bigger than expected loss. If an agent (Wakalah) is used then the fund is further divided to provide a clear delineation for the Wakalah fees.

---

[256] Ayub *op cit* p 422

[257] Ayub *op cit* p 422

[258] Waqf is the retention of a property for the benefit of a charitable or humanitarian objective or for members of one's own family. The relevant feature here is that the ownership of the Waqf property is transferred in perpetuity. Waqf property cannot be sold. The idea of Waqf extends to money as property. Once donated to the Takaful pool's protection part, the money is managed by the pool not the individual's in the pool – you can't take your money back. However, money in the savings and investment part can be used to generate a profit.

Takaful Re

As in the conventional system it is possible to arrange Takaful to insure other Takaful. This is re-insurance. Agreed fees are paid into a re-Takaful by other Takaful funds to protect one of the funds in the event of losses.

Waqf is the Preferred Model for Takaful

Takaful is an area of intense research among Shari'ah scholars. As a result, various models for Takaful's practical implementation have been proposed. The preferred model is that of a "Waqf model or a combination of Wakalah with Waqf". The jurists believe that this "is the best basis of evolving a practical Takaful system in line with Shari'ah principles."[259] Practically, it works as follows:

> *Contributions of the participants, appropriate to the risk of the participants/assets, are divided into two parts: one as donation to the Takaful fund and the other for investment on the basis of Mudarabah. The donation part always remains with the Waqf. Operational costs like re-Takaful, claims, etc. are met from the fund. The underwriting surplus or loss belongs to the fund, which can be distributed to the beneficiaries of the Waqf, kept as a reserve or reinvested to the benefit of the Waqf. There is no obligation to distribute the surplus. Rules for management fees, distribution of profit, creation of reserves, the procedure, extent or limit of compensation to the policyholders are decided beforehand.*

Takaful Industry Successful but More Work is Needed

The Islamic Insurance Company of Sudan opened in 1979 and Takaful has enjoyed significant growth since then. Takaful insurance is available to meet the needs of all sectors of the economy; for individuals and companies, over short and long terms and the needs of different groups. There are even Takaful companies enjoying limited success in non-Muslim countries. There are, however, factors limiting its growth and its chance to compete with conventional insurance. Ayub notes the following[260]:

- The huge investment required to compete with the conventional insurance industry
- The changes required in regulatory requirements, as seen in the case of Malaysia, to allow Takaful to compete on equal terms with the conventional industry
- Belief by Muslims that insurance is un-Islamic or that a Shari'ah-compliant alternative is unavailable.
- Lack of qualified professionals and/or training within Islamic Financial Institutions

---

[259] Ayub *op cit* p 423
[260] Ayub *op cit* p 426

Table Comparing Takaful and Conventional Insurance

The following comparison table is not exhaustive but will give a flavour of the issues that are important for Shari'ah compliance.

Conventional Insurance	Takaful
Risk is transferred to one party	Risk shared among all members of the pool
Policyholders pay premiums against unknown risk (the insurance company has this information but keeps it to itself)	Policy holders aware of the risks as they manage the fund for themselves or appoint a trusted agent to do this
A small premium could return large payment (Riba) without an appropriate risk	Riba avoided as the insured are putting their own non-refundable money at risk
Profit-driven: premiums are set in a competitive context with adequacy of cover not the foremost consideration	Pricing mechanism means subscribers recover any excess due to over-pricing. This refund comes from investment or UWS[261]

---

[261] Underwriting surplus (UWS) as opposed to UWL

PART FIVE – Conclusion and Answers

This conclusion tries to answer the questions about Islamic Finance that were asked at the beginning.

Answers

The book started with some questions. It should end with some answers.

1.   **Would the current economic crisis have occurred if the world had been using IF?**

It is surely impossible to say if a global economic crisis would have occurred under one system or another. Perhaps more powerful and sophisticated computer models could provide clues to our thinking. I think that, certainly with a prohibition on interest and uncertainty (not the uncertainty accepted as business risk), the current crisis as it was could not have occurred. However, as always, this would only result if all of the actors in the global financial system were to play by the rules. The behaviour of many financial players, from Lehman Brothers running the gamut of reputable Wall Street and City of London institutions appears to have been based on a "Let's see if we can get away with it and bet on the fact that the regulators will:

a.   not be in a position to stop us

b.   not understand what is happening, as the system is unbelievably complex and fast-moving

c.   concerned that interference might be the trigger for worse problems

Of course elements of all of these issues were present when the system did crash and the investigations started. Of course if those who hold the wealth (rich investors, pension funds, insurance companies and banks that have borrowed cheaply from governments) feel that they would not be rewarded appropriately for lending their money they would not necessarily put it into projects that would see the growth of economies all over the world. Like it or not the interest and uncertainty filled model that we have used has opened up massive opportunities and has improved the lives of billions. It's not immediately clear how an IF system would provide a basis for growth that was adequately rapid or any less prone to the constant risks that attend being an active part of a growing global economy. It's not just inflation that reduces the value of money. Scarcity of essential resources will do the same thing to the man on the street.

2.   **Would it have been possible for the rapid growth in the world economy (or even that of Europe after WW2) without the use of interest?**

The basis on which money has been put forward by those who currently hold it (ie where there is a surplus) to those who would wish to borrow it is a very simple calculation. By adding on a known amount the lender can protect himself from changes in the economy while his money is locked away in a binding contract. The amount of interest to be received and the time before the capital will be returned is known with the two main risks clearly understood:

a.   default by the borrower

b.   inflation (which has as one source possibly the interest payable on a loan and as another the increase in price of items due to their scarcity. Both of which can be mitigated by careful choice of the tenor and coupon rate of the loan (whether this is a government or corporate bond for example)

There is no doubt that some of the excessive rates charged by Western financiers to Third World countries should be, and indeed have been, reviewed. The value of money as a marker of value has been changing throughout its history and not all of this change is directly related to interest charged on loans.

3.   **Would not charging interest be a hindrance or a help in a modern global economy?**

Encouraging people to enter into complex partnership for the creation of profit-making possibilities takes time and needs a level of trust to be established between partners. It needs the financier to have a view of and perhaps even assay in running the business that is seeking a loan. Not every business wants this someone else involved in its decision-making processes. The owners are happy to take the money, paid the agreed price for the money and then move the business on by themselves. Both sides run risks but they are generally easy to understand. The business owes money to a known institution or person and must repay it as a cost against the business. The lender runs the risk that the business will fail but is protected to a reasonable extent by the business owner's desire to keep a good reputation and to hold onto resources that may have been put up as collateral against the loan and, of course, the law.

4.   **Does an IF system have any advantages that are not found in the current, diverse, global financial system?** The system has at its core a professed socio-economic aim supported by an Islamic belief in social justice with respect to wealth. The prohibition on interest (Riba) is to ensure that:

> **"...(wealth) does not make a circuit between the wealthy among you" (Quran 59:7)**

This is clearly aimed at ensuring that wealth cannot be increased solely by the possession of money. Money as a marker of value is to be used to increase social justice through honest trading and an increase in wealth that is not based solely on time. Working and living within a system that has justice as aim is, without doubt, a highly desirable aim and one that should be striven for. However, there are many people and institutions that exist outside Islamic Finance that have similar aims. They do this within the context of an interest-based system.

5.   **Does an IF system have any disadvantages that are not found in the current, diverse, global financial system?** The prohibitions and encouragements in the Islamic Finance system are religiously-founded. Obviously, it is not necessary, although it may well be sufficient, to believe in punishment in the afterlife to want to be an honest member of society who is willing to put the interests of less well-off members of society higher up a personal agenda. The system has lot of checks and balances and relies a great deal on the social aspect of a Muslim's life, but these restrictions may limit what can be achieved when the system is in competition with the incumbent Western model. For example, many Muslims who have moved to

the West have bought houses using mortgages from banks and building societies for which they have had to pay interest. It would be impossible for most people to own property otherwise as there has not been a Shari'ah-based alternative available. Western interest-based mortgages are uncomplicated (in general), easy to understand and are easily available. To suggest that people using them when there is no alternative will suffer in the afterlife as a result of wanting to improve their own lot and that of their children in life seems, even for some Muslims, hard to accept. It will take some time for Shari'ah-compliant mortgages to be readily available in the UK for example, although the situation is changing rapidly. The Quran does allow that Muslims who cease to use haram products such as interest-based mortgages will not burn in hell but will still be answerable to Allah upon their deaths. The slow pace of progress will always be a disadvantage as the required Shari'ah-based checks are exhaustive in nature.

6.   **Is the elimination of paying interest the most effective way to achieve or ensure social justice?** Setting aside the outrageous behaviour of companies like Wonga (whose very existence is a testament to corporate greed), this will always be an issue for many Muslim bankers and traders who, in an increasingly fast-moving, interest-based and complex financial environment, are declaring their willingness to be handicapped by their professed religious beliefs. Not charging or paying interest makes the whole process of accessing money for whatever reason (social or otherwise) slower and more complex. This may prevent them acting quickly to help in situations in which other beliefs that they hold require that they act.

There is, of course, nothing wrong with handicapping oneself in order to change the world for the better; many people have used their riches and religious convictions to benefit the less well-off members of societies, for example through trusts, foundations and personal charitable giving. There are numerous companies that were founded in Victorian England by families of Quakers (The Religious Society of Friends), for example, the Reckitts, Rowntrees and Cadburys who invested their money in areas deemed for the social good (social housing, confectionery etc) as opposed to weapons of war. Muslims are not allowed to invest in haram products, including arms, alcohol, pork meat or pornography and they must adhere to strict rules about what money is and how it can be loaned out even without a strict legal framework. The Quakers are pacifist, pragmatic and campaign tirelessly for improved social justice but nowhere in their work is the elimination of paying interest considered a priority let alone a religious requirement. Where the paying of interest is having a significant deleterious effect it needs to be reviewed, for example, Third World Debt, the campaigns for which have been run by people with significant and well-known religious convictions such as Gordon Brown, the former UK Prime Minister.

7.   **Would governments be able to finance large projects over many years in an interest-free environment?** A lender is not going to invest his investors' money (pension funds, people's life savings etc) for up to 30 years without some return being given that would allow his investors to live – that is why they invest in the first place. One IF alternative is the complex set of

Shari'ah-compliant contracts taking the form of a Sukuk. These Sukuk mean that the investors invest the money in the real-world economy with its attendant risk of failure and loss of funds. The aim of a pension fund is to reduce to almost zero the risk of loss for people who cannot afford to lose their money; pensioners, people with low income etc. Government bond with their sovereign-based guarantee form the bedrock of low-to-zero risk based investments with fixed returns. It would not be in the interest of social justice if the most vulnerable members of society had to bear the brunt of a failed infrastructure project. Even if the low interest payments they are currently receiving are squeezing their incomes, the guarantee of some fixed return at interest for the money they have invested will allow them to pay their rent, buy energy and food and rest well at night. It was unbridled greed and the madness of crowds that caused the system to crash and the global financial crisis hit Muslim funds just as much as Western funds. Greed and speculation over luxury accommodation in Dubai caused the property crash there in 2009 not the charging of interest if that occurred during the financing of the project.

8.   **Is there an ethical argument that would push people to adopt, if not all of the elements of IF, then at least some of the 'good' ideas that it proposes?** The finance system under Shari'ah is declared to be an ethical system that emphasises the use of wealth for the betterment of society. There is strong social and religious pressure to treat business as a way to ensure social justice through the avoidance of Riba (interest), Gharar (uncertainty) and Maisir (games of chance). Honest traders are to be treated on a par with the prophets. The giving of alms to charity, the payment for a poor person's pilgrimage to Mecca and the role of the state in the formulation of price controls in a distorted market are all aimed at sharing the benefits of being a Muslim, being part of the ummah. Certainly, the creation **and application** of strict laws regarding uncertainty in a sales contract or the deleterious effect of the occasionally casino-like global financial system can only improve people's confidence in how the system works. The system must be made to work for everyone and not just the top 1%. Without doubt there are elements in IF that will help to achieve this all other things being equal. Unfortunately, all other things are not equal. As a financial system, Islamic Finance has to compete against the current one and it has to be able to meet all the needs of everyone using it. Whether or not this is possible is a question that is almost impossible to answer. It may meet the needs of those Muslims who are, as Ayub dramatically puts it, 'waging a war against Allah' but there is much that works well in the current system also – when that system is allowed to work effectively with appropriate controls appropriately enforced.

9.   **What if we didn't call the ideas Islamic Finance?** The underpinning of the restriction on interest is a clear prohibition stemming directly from the Islamic Holy Book, the Quran. Without the social pressure inherent in Islam or the threat of burning in hell that is faced by the faithful Muslim, it may be difficult, as the Catholic Church and governments have found out through the centuries, to eliminate interest as a means of

encouraging those with an excess of money to lend it to those who need it to allow them to create wealth of their own. The elimination of uncertainty in contracts and the reduction of the casino-like behaviour of the modern financial markets is not a uniquely Islamic idea and both are already subject to legislation in different countries and in supranational entities such as the EU. As to whether the legislation can stop determined 'self-aggrandizers' from looking for loopholes or just engaging in plain fraudulent behaviour is a matter that should cause us to worry about human nature. You cannot legislate for human nature. What the system is called is not important, how we behave towards each other as human beings is. We have a long road ahead of us.

Islamic Finance may provide a route for some as they travel down that road.

BOOKS

Dogan I, Michailidou A (2008) Trading in prehistory and protohistory: Perspectives from the eastern Aegean and beyond

Ayub Muhammed (2007) Introduction to Islamic Finance. John Wiley London

Causse-Broquet, Geneviève (2009) La Finance Islamique, Revue Banque Edition

Kidwai, Azra (2004) Islam, Roli Books

Lombard, Maurice (2003) The Golden Age of Islam, Markus Wien

www.ingramcontent.com/pod-product-compliance
Lightning Source LLC
Chambersburg PA
CBHW032024170526

45157CB00002B/852